On the Trail of the Real
ST GEORGE

OLIVER HAYES

info@BretwaldaBooks.com

To receive an e-catalogue of our
complete range of books send an email
to info@BretwaldaBooks.com

ISBN 978-1-907791-52-9

Bretwalda Books Ltd

Contents

Introduction 4

Chapter 1 *The Martyr* 6

Chapter 2 *A Dark Age Saint* 22

Chapter 3 *On Crusade* 32

Chapter 4 *Enter The Dragon* 44

Chapter 5 *A Very English Saint* 60

Chapter 6 *The Obscure Years* 76

Chapter 7 *St George Resurgent* 84

Index 96

Introduction

As flags go, it is stunning. A blood red cross on a white background is instantly recognisable, easily produced and clear enough to be spotted a mile away. It is a flag that England has made its own.

These days, you can see St George's flag almost anywhere. When England is playing in an international football competition, they are everywhere. They flutter from cars, being carried on plastic struts that attach to the car windows. Larger versions are nailed to wooden poles lashed to builders' vans and trucks. Houses have flags flying from windows, garages and garden fences. Shops are festooned with them and pubs are swathed in St George's flags, St George's buntings and St George's posters.

The imagination of modern marketing men has been let loose on the once simple flag of St George. Breweries put their logos into the white quarters of the flag to link their product to the ubiquitous flags. Other flags are decorated with a silhouette of a mounted knight in armour piercing a fierce dragon with a lance. Some combine the coat of arms of England with the flag of St George by displaying three lions on the flag. Advertisements show jocular knights in armour and a surcoat displaying the flag enjoying a wide variety of products seeking to gain sales by being linked to the patron saint of England.

St George and his flag have entered the public life of England in a big way. Fully grown men dress up as St George to go to football matches or to slip down the pub to watch English cricketers take on foreign rivals on giant television screens. His flag is emblazoned on supermarket packs to show that the apples, steaks or lager within was produced in England.

In part this modern obsession with St George has got a lot to do with the marvels of modern manufacturing. Time was when flags were expensive things to buy. Coloured dyes that would remain true in sun, rain and wind were pricey to make and costly to fix on cloth. Now with new synthetic fabrics and artificial dyes, a pound or two will buy you a colourful flag that would previously have set you back half a day's wages. Flags, costumes and outfits are cheap enough to be bought, used and discarded without much cost.

But there is also something about St George himself that captures the English mind. In the public imagination, St George is a bold, fearless and hearty chap. He thinks nothing of grabbing sword or lance to rush into battle against a ferocious dragon to save a pretty damsel. No doubt he would be just as ready to hurl himself into battle to slaughter foreign enemies of England. And nobody can be in much doubt that he would celebrate his victory with a vast platter of sausages, steaks and chips washed down with a beer or two, while belting out a singalong chant with his mates.

St George's image is decidedly male and working class. In these days when politicians tell us that "we are all middle class now", submerge England into a bureaucratic European Union and seek to embrace a touchy-feely empathy with the world, St George gallops out on his white horse to remind us of a very different England. When the football World Cup comes around it is Council estates and areas of smaller houses that are festooned with red and white, and it is white vans that carry the largest flags.

Big, bold, brave and determined to enjoy himself while cheerfully slaughtering his enemies, St George is seen in much the same way as the English like to think of themselves.

But what was the real St George like? How has he come to embody the more robust virtues of the English? To find the answers we must set out on the trail of the real St George.

Chapter 1

The Martyr

If everyone in England is familiar with the St George of heroic legend, what of the real St George? Was there such a man? Did he really exist? The figure of the real St George peers at us from more than seventeen centuries ago. He looks out from a very different world than the one we know today. He is very different too. There is no dragon, no lance, no red cross, no shining armour and no prancing steed. It would be difficult to imagine a man more different from the St George of modern imagination. And yet there is a direct link over the centuries from the shadowy figure whom we can see all those centuries ago to the gallant hero of modern days.

The real St George lived in the later days of the Roman Empire. This was before the economic collapse came that would undermine the ancient world, before the barbarian invasions came to smash the established order and destroy the greatest empire the world had ever seen. He lived in a time when Rome ruled the civilised Western World, when the imperial government was ordered under Consuls who had sat in the sacred seat in Rome for over eight centuries. The economy was secure, the society solid and peace spread over the world.

Although so much about the Roman Empire was secure and ancient, there were dramatic changes taking place. The Empire had recently been divided between rival emperors, each claiming to be the one true ruler. Battles had been fought, senior figures assassinated and long distance trade disrupted. Those disorders had been put down, but their effects were still felt. Even more disruptive for ordinary people leading ordinary lives were the religious changes sweeping the Empire. It was these changes that brought George his fame, his glory and his death.

Belief in the traditional gods of Rome was declining, and had been for some time. The familiar Roman goddesses and gods of Jupiter, Mars and Minerva were worshipped in public and ceremonies often involved formal state events or officials. While there were more local deities and some local family divinities, the spiritual life of the western world in the 3rd century seems to have been undergoing a crisis. What seems to have been a vague widespread sense of spiritual emptiness was met in many ways.

Foremost among the pagan answers were what were known collectively as the "mystery cults". These cults were a varied group, but

A stone relief showing the god Mithras sacrificing a bull. The cult of Mithras was popular in Rome at the time that Christianity was gaining strength. *Cristian Chirita*

they shared some essential characteristics. The cults were each dedicated to a particular deity, for whom claims of supremacy or primary importance were made. The cults held their ceremonies in private and devotees were sworn to secrecy as to what went on. Those wishing to join a cult had to promise not only secrecy, but usually a range of other dedications to the chosen deity. Outsiders were not permitted to join the rituals.

Among the more popular of the mystery cults were those of the grain goddess Demeter (dubbed the Eleusian Mysteries as the cult began at Eleusis in Greece), the wine god Dionysus whose rituals involved drunken dances and rhythmic music, and the Egyptian mother goddess Isis. The Persian solar deity Mithras had a cult that was hugely popular in the army, and was perhaps the most widespread of the cults.

Another religion that was at first seen by many in the Roman world as yet another mystery cult was also spreading fast. This was Christianity. It shared with the mystery cults the presence of an initiation ceremony, rituals that only adherents could join and claims of primacy for the God involved. For the Roman state, what marked Christianity out was that Christians believed that their God was the only God, not simply the most important among many. This meant that Christians refused to join the public acts of worship for the state gods and denied the sacred underpinnings on which Imperial power rested. For the most part Christians and government officials were content to rub along, finding a way to compromise religious belief with state demands. As Christianity spread, however, conflicts became increasingly numerous and serious.

The pagan Roman Emperor Diocletian ruled from 284 to 305. His crackdown on Christians was part of a wider effort to control groups outside of the imperial system.

The Martyr

In 284 a successful army officer named Diocletian was elected to be emperor by the army after the Emperor Numerian was murdered. Talented, efficient and ruthless, Diocletian set about reforming the Roman government and army with a skill and passion that had not been seen for decades. Among his reforms was the rejuvenation of the worship of the official state gods of Rome, and of the formal ceremonies that accompanied them. Diocletian saw the revived state religion as a way to unite the various nationalities within the Roman Empire and to give them a common purpose. The idea worked well for nearly everyone – apart from the Christians. In 297 Diocletian decreed that anyone who did not join in with the official state rituals would be banned from working for the government.

The early Christian leader and bishop, Eusebius of Caesarea was the first man to write about the martyr who suffered death on 23 April 303.

Meanwhile, a long-running war with Persia was going badly and pagan officers in the army blamed a cabal of Christian officers. Moreover a group of senior pagan priests had become jealous of funds and bequests that were going to Christian churches instead of to pagan temples. They pointed out to Diocletian that bequests to pagan temples usually included a share for the Emperor, while those to Christian churches did not. The final straw came at Antioch in the autumn of 302 when a Christian deacon named Romanus interrupted official pagan rituals and started a fight that stopped the ceremonies being completed. The interruption rendered the rituals invalid.

Diocletian was furious. He ordered Romanus to have his tongue cut out and then to be thrown into prison. Diocletian then travelled to consult the powerful oracle of the god Apollo at nearby Didyma. Apollo, speaking through his priests, told the emperor that he could not offer advice "due to the impious ones" in imperial service.

Diocletian at once ordered all civil servants and army officers to take an oath sacred to the pagan gods or to resign. Many Christians left their jobs, but that was not enough.

On 23 February 303, Diocletian ordered that the newly-built cathedral in the city of Nicomedia be destroyed. Nicomedia was close to Didyma so the new church was held to have offended Apollo — and in any case Diocletian had a palace in Nicomedia and had no wish to look out on a Christian church from his bedroom window. Other churches were to be stripped of treasures and the wealth handed over to the imperial treasury. Christians were also banned from speaking in courts, taking part in government business or otherwise having an official existence in the eyes of the state – even slaves fared better.

The Greek god Apollo. All the earliest references to St George portray him as being vehemently opposed to the worship of this pagan god.

Five days later the imperial palace caught fire. Inevitably, Diocletian blamed a Christian conspiracy and ordered the execution of several leading Christians.

With much of his palace in ruins, Diocletian left the Eastern provinces of the empire for Rome, then went campaigning against barbarian tribes in the Danube Valley. In 305 he suddenly retired, going to live in a fortified palace overlooking the Adriatic, and died in 311. With

Diocletian gone, the persecutions lost their impetus as many local officials were either Christians themselves or found the religious killings distasteful. In the more relaxed atmosphere Christianity revived. Those who had been executed were treated as honoured martyrs. Their bones were dug up and placed in shrines or reburied under monuments that commemorated their actions and deaths. When Constantine lifted all restrictions on Christianity the number of churches and Christians boomed. This was clearly an interesting time to be a Christian.

If some changes were already happening to the Roman world, others were on their way. In the barbarian invasions and the turmoil that followed something more than 99% of all written records were destroyed, either deliberately or through neglect. This widespread destruction can make it very difficult to be certain exactly what

The Roman Emperor Constantine, who ruled the entire
Roman Empire from 312 to 337, paid for a shrine to be built
to cover the tomb of St George at Lydda.

happened in the ancient world. Many aspects of Roman history and society remain obscure to us today simply because the written records were destroyed. There is little that can be said with any real certainty — there are different versions of events even in the oldest sources — and it can be difficult to sort out truth from legend. As a rule, however, it is usually best to start with the oldest written sources on the grounds that they are more likely to be accurate, or at least not to include any information that would have sounded obviously wrong to the people reading it.

The oldest reference to St George is almost certainly to be found in a History of the Church written by Bishop Eusebius of Caesarea in about 322. It is worth noting in the light of later events that Caesarea was the main city in the province of Cappadocia (now Kapadokya in

Medieval paintings at the Kremikovtsi Monastery, Bulgaria, showing the life of St George. The central image shows St George holding a dead serpent beneath his foot to symbolise his victory over paganism.

Turkey). Eusebius is known to have been a close friend of the Romanus who had interrupted the pagan rituals of Diocletian, which no doubt coloured his views of Diocletian and the persecutions of Christians he ordered. Eusebius survived the persecutions and in 324 saw the Christian Emperor Constantine become the undisputed ruler of the whole empire. Bishop Eusebius promptly wrote a biography of Constantine that was a master class in sycophantic flattery.

He had reasons to want to gain the favour of the new supreme ruler. Constantine was aware that there were dozens of different Christian traditions within the Roman Empire. Bishops did not co-operate with each other and often argued fiercely about doctrine, ceremony and which books were genuine histories of Christ and which were not. As soon as he gained power, Constantine called a meeting of all the Christian bishops to take place at Nicaea (now Iznik in Turkey) to thrash out all the disagreements. The Council of Nicaea produced the Nicaean Creed, a way to calculate when Easter fell each year and issued rulings on various theological points. One of these was on the relationship between the three persons of the Holy Trinity — the Father, the Son and the Holy Ghost.

Bishop Eusebius found himself on the losing side and, since he did not accept the Nicaean rulings, on the wrong side of Constantine. If he had not been such a good historian he may well have been ousted from his bishopric, or even condemned for heresy. As it was, Eusebius spent the rest of his life trying to make things up to Constantine.

In Book VII of his History of the Church, Eusebius gives details of the great persecution of Christianity by the Emperor Diocletian which began in 302 and lasted, off and on, until 311. Among those recorded by Eusebius as being killed was "A man of the greatest distinction", who was sentenced to death by Emperor Diocletian in Nicomedia on 23 April 303. Eusebius does not mention the name of the man, nor any details of his crime, execution or career. The context, however, implies that this man had tried to stop the destruction of the cathedral in Nicomedia (now Izmit in Turkey), and that it was for this opposition to an imperial order that he was killed.

In about the year 345 or thereabouts a church was built in the town of Shakka, Syria. The original church has long since gone, but the door lintel has survived. On it are carved words that translate as "This is the house of the holy and triumphant martyr George, and of the holy ones who suffered martyrdom alongside him." It is the earliest reference to a martyr named George.

A few years later, another Syrian church was dedicated to the martyr George. Unlike the small chapel at Shakka, the structure at Adhra was a substantial stone building, having previously been a pagan temple. The cult statue of the pagan god was torn down and dragged outside to be smashed up – a fate that was shared by many pagan statues of enormous artistic merit. In its place was erected a stone altar on which was carved the following inscription in Greek:

"This home of demons has become a house of God. A light has shone in the place where darkness held sway. Where there were sacrifices to idols there are now songs of angels. Where God was angry he is now content. A lover of Christ, John the noble man, son of Diomedes, has paid with his own money to create as a gift to God a building that is suitable for the purpose. He has placed within this structure a relic of the splendidly triumphant and most holy martyr George who appeared to John himself, not in a dream but as a real vision."

Both these inscriptions were carved when people who had been alive during the persecution of Diocletian would still be alive and able to remember what had happened. Neither of them specifically links the martyr George to the man killed on 23 April 303, but they do make it clear that this George was highly respected and revered in Syria at this time.

Within a century, however, documents were being written that state that the martyr George was being commemorated on 23 April, which was believed to be the anniversary of his death. Moreover, it was recorded that the Emperor Constantine, no less, had given money to build a shrine over the tomb of the martyr George. The shrine was built at Lydda (now Lod in Israel) in the Plain of Sharon.

The ruins of the Temple of Apollo at Didyma. It was
the priests at this temple who persuaded Emperor Diocletian
to begin his persecution of the Christians.

There has been much speculation over the form this shrine took. We do not know how much money Constantine gave nor do any ruins remain. It has been suggested that the shrine was, in fact, the former Temple of Apollo that had been stripped of its pagan statues and reconsecrated as a Christian church dedicated to St George. This would not have been a very unusual event at the time when Christianity was replacing paganism. It would explain why the Church of St George at Lydda was later said to be large and magnificent. If it were a converted Temple of Apollo, the Church of St George may well have continued some remnants of its pagan past. In particular, the church may have retained the plinths on which a statue of Apollo had once stood. We know from elsewhere that plinths of pagan gods were often decorated with attributes of the god in question. One of the key symbols of Apollo was the gigantic snake Pythia, and snakes were not uncommonly carved on plinths and bases of statues of Apollo. Perhaps

A bust of the Roman Emperor Constantine. The accession of this, the first Christian Emperor of Rome, transformed the religious life of the empire.

one such carving remained in the church. In any case there would have been a strong link between George who had denounced Apollo and Apollo's snake. It may have been this that first established the iconography of St George defeating a serpent.

Others have sought to find a link between George and a gigantic snake in Constantine's gift. Several Christian officials at this time used the symbol of a Christian banner, a labaraum, spearing a snake to symbolise the triumph of Christianity over paganism. Constantine is known to have produced at least one coin bearing the symbol and is thought to have used it elsewhere. It has been suggested that when Constantine built the church over the tomb of St George he may have included a statue or relief of himself to commemorate the act. This would certainly be standard practice at the time as patrons who spent money on a sacred building usually wanted later visitors to know whom to thank. If Constantine had decorated the church with a carving of himself it is possible that he may have shown himself spearing a serpent, as he did on his coins. It is argued that later visitors to the church may have seen the carving of the emperor and mistaken it for one of St George. Thus the martyr may have been linked to a dragon-like creature by accident.

It is an interesting theory, but there is no evidence at all to support it. We have no idea what Constantine's church looked like nor whether it featured an image of the emperor, be he in serpent-slaying pose or not. It would also establish a link between George and a serpent. There is no more evidence for this symbol in the original church at Lydda, any more than there is for a Pythia carving, but that is not to say that such a carving was not there.

Taken together these very early sources make it clear that a man named George was killed because of his Christian faith, probably on 23 April 303. This George had obviously made a big impression on his contemporaries for he had at least two churches dedicated to him within living memory of his death and a shrine or chapel was built over his tomb on the instructions of the Emperor Constantine. No other martyr of the date can claim such devotion.

Sometime around the year 400, the date is in dispute, a Christian scribe living in what was then Nobatia (now Qasr Ibrim, Egypt) wrote out brief accounts of the lives of a number of martyrs. Among them was the martyr George and this account has become known as the "Egyptian Life" of St George.

According to the unknown scribe of Nobatia, George had been born in Egypt during the reign of the Emperor Aurelian (270-275). George's father was a pagan named Gerontius who worked for the Roman government in an unspecified capacity. Gerontius had originally come from Cappadocia. At this date both Cappadocia and Nobatia were part of the far flung Roman Empire and officials were often moved from one province to another by the government. George's mother was a Christian named Polychronia. She had George secretly baptised, and as he grew up taught him about Jesus Christ.

According to this version of his life, George completed his education, and then got a job in the Imperial government through the influence of his father. He later moved to Lydda in the province of Syria where he was promoted to a senior, but unspecified, government position. The local governor was a pagan who suddenly announced that only pagans could remain in Lydda. George spoke out against the instruction, denouncing the god Apollo in furious terms in front of the pagan governor during an official function. George was at once arrested and tortured in public. His feet were forced into metal boots lined with spikes, but he calmly began preaching to the assembled crowd on the benefits of Christianity. George was then tied to a wooden stake and whipped, but again he ignored his pain to talk about Christ. The Archangel Michael then appeared, blessed George and healed his wounds. Restored to health, George returned to preaching the faith of Christianity, and converted many onlookers. Even the pagan governor's wife renounced her pagan gods. George then led the mob of newly converted Christians to attack and sack the Temple of Apollo that dominated the main square in Lydda. The governor responded by sending in soldiers who attacked the mob, killing many of them, and captured George. Dragged in front of the pagan governor again, George condemned Apollo in forthright terms. George was then dragged out on to the steps of the Temple of Apollo and beheaded by order of the pagan governor.

This version of George's life is the earliest that has survived. It would seem to fit reasonably well the known facts of the persecution of Diocletian. It is interesting that George is said to attack Apollo, when it was the priests of Apollo at Didyma

St George is led to execution in a fresco from Padua completed in about 1380.

who spurred Diocletian into action. Similarly the death of this George is located at Lydda, where Constantine raised a shrine over the tomb of the martyr George – so presumably we are dealing with one and the same man. If George had been born around 270, he would have been over thirty years old by 303 which is a reasonable age to be a fairly senior civil servant at the time. It is worth noting that the scribe makes a great point of mentioning that George converts to Christianity the wife of the pagan governor. The woman here is a shadowy figure of no apparent relevance to the story, but she is mentioned several times as if she is somehow important. The conversion of a high-born lady would remain a permanent fixture of the various stories about St George.

A slightly later version of George's life was written sometime before 480, perhaps as early as 420, in one of the eastern provinces. It is sometimes dubbed the Syrian Life to distinguish it from the version

19

The Greek god Silenus – famed for his drunkeness – was a leading figure in the worship of the god Dionysus, whose worship was an early rival to Christianity.

written in Egypt, though it is also sometimes called the Vienna Palimpsest as it is stored in Vienna and is written on a reused piece of parchment (a palimpsest). The work opens by stating that the facts within it have been verified by a man named Pasicrates who had known George personally and had witnessed many of the events described. This statement need not be taken too seriously as such claims were often made by writers at this date to lend credence to their tales. On the other hand, it may well be that the manuscript we have was based in part on an earlier work that had in fact been verified by Pasicrates.

In this version George was born in Cappadocia and joined the Roman army as a young man. He proved to be a talented soldier and rose to become a senior officer. He was serving as deputy to the general Anatolius in Syria when the local governor Dadianos ordered that everyone had to sacrifice to the pagan god Apollo. George refused and publicly denounced the false god Apollo. In this version, George is once again subjected to tortures which are even more inventive and painful than those described by the Nobatian scribe. The tortures occupy rather more of this document, and have more fantastic details. George was actually killed three times under torture — the first time when his back was broken on a wheel, the second time when Dadianos poured molten lead down his throat and third time when he was whipped until his ribs shone white in the sun. Each time the Archangel Michael appeared and restored George to perfect health. This impressive display converted to Christianity the general Anatolius and a princess named Alexandra, both of whom are promptly beheaded by order of Dadianos. George himself was then beheaded and this time stayed dead.

The Syrian Life of George is quite obviously a highly fictionalised version that was written to emphasise the sufferings of the martyr and the power of God to overcome them. The lengthy accounts of the tortures undergone by George make for gruesome reading and a modern reader could be forgiven for feeling queasy. Behind these invented details, however, there can still be discerned a basic framework that had a basis in reality. As in the Egyptian Life, George is said to be of Cappadocian origins and to be working for the Roman government in Syria. He falls foul of orders to perform pagan sacrifices to Apollo and is martyred. The Syrian life is the earliest time that George is described as being a soldier. The earlier Egyptian Life had merely said he worked for the Roman government in some way.

If these two accounts are correct that George was born into a noble Cappadocian family, it would explain why Bishop Eusebius had been interested in his martyrdom.

Although the very earliest sources for St George are partial, often vague and occasionally inconsistent they do produce a fairly clear picture of the Real St George. Exactly how this martyr of the Christian faith in the face of a resurgent paganism in the Roman Empire became a beer-swilling, football-mad patron saint of England remains to be seen. It is a twisting and at times confusing trail to follow.

Chapter 2

A Dark Age Saint

As the Roman World descended into chaos in the 5th century, the fame of George the Great Martyr spread and strengthened. At this distance in time it is difficult to see exactly what it was about George that ensured that his name spread beyond Lydda and its immediate area. There were plenty of other martyrs being venerated at the time, and most remained restricted to the place where they had lived and died. George was different. Perhaps it was his steadfast faith or his aggression or perhaps the increasingly imaginative tortures he was said to have suffered. Whatever it was, the veneration of George moved out from Lydda to many parts of the Roman world.

A very different fate was accorded to the veneration of another Christian martyred by a local Roman governor. This saint will re-enter our story some seventeen centuries later, but in the 4th and 5th centuries he was just a typical martyr. Alban was a pagan Roman citizen living in the city of Verulamium (now St Albans in Hertfordshire) who was converted to Christianity by a nomadic Christian cleric who had come from Caerleon where he had been ministering to Christians in the army base there. It is recorded in later accounts that the priest's name was Amphibalus, but as this means simply "the cloaked one" it may be a nickname or alias.

Orders were then sent out by the Roman governor that all Christian priests were to be rounded up for execution. Alban swapped clothes with the priest and was arrested in his stead. Once the priest had had

Built around 650 in the Greek quarter of Rome, San Giorgio Velabro stands on the site of a Roman temple and was built largely with the fabric of that pagan structure. *Zello*

enough time to get away, Alban revealed his own identity presumably in the hope of being freed. Instead the local magistrate was so angry at having been tricked that he ordered Alban to be executed instead. Alban was led out of the city toward the nearby Holmhurst Hill for execution. On the way they had to cross the River Ver, but the bridge was crowded with people and there was no way across. Alban knelt in prayer, whereupon the waters parted allowing him and his guards to walk across the dry river bed. The procession moved on and when it reached the top of the hill, Alban again knelt in prayer. At which point a soldier sliced his head off with a sword.

The date of the martyrdom has traditionally been fixed in 303, the same year that St George was put to death. However more recently scholars have suggested that the execution may have taken place in

The church of Sankt Georg stands on the island of Reichenau in Lake Constance in southern Germany. This monastic site was founded in 724 by Christian monks fleeing the Moslem invasion of Spain.

208. One copy of an early document states that Alban was executed by orders of "Caesar Severus", and the Emperor Severus was in Britain in 208. Others suggest that the phrase "Caesar Severus" was simply a mistake for a generic term for "severe emperor", in which case Alban was more likely to have died in the Persecution of Diocletian.

Whenever he died, the local Christian community erected a small memorial on the site of Alban's execution within a decade or so of the event. That memorial became first a church by around 500 and then a monastery in 793. That monastery survived until the dissolution of the monasteries in the 1530s, after which the abbey church became the parish church for the town.

St Alban soon became a leading British saint, his shrine being a popular centre for pilgrimage. During the time that the pagan Angles and Saxons were busy converting post-Roman Britain into England the difficulties of getting to St Alban's shrine were a frequent cause for complaint among the Christian British. Despite this fame within Britain, St Alban never became either famous or much revered beyond the island. Such local fame was typical for martyrs at this time.

George, however, was riding high. In about 490 King Clovis of the

Franks founded a monastery of St George in the town of Baralle, now in northeastern France. Emperor Justinian of Byzantium founded a church in his honour in Armenia at much the same time.

The spreading cult of St George almost fell foul of Papal politics in the year 494. Pope Gelasius was under pressure from the people of Rome. He had been pope for only two years at this point, but had already gained a reputation as a hardline enforcer of orthodox doctrine and as a vociferous champion of the primacy of the Bishop of Rome, or pope, over other bishops. Then, in January 494, he wrote to Senator Andromachus instructing him to ban the popular festival of the Lupercalia. This two-day celebration was pagan in origin, having been instituted in the earliest days of Rome as a way to ritually cleanse and renew the city, while preparing it for the coming year. The pagan festival had featured sacrifices, feasting and lighthearted frolicking through the streets when young men ran around lashing out with rawhide thongs to bring fertility to young women. By 494 the pagan sacrifices had gone, but the feasting and chases through the streets remained. Andromachus refused to ban what he saw as a harmless street party.

In the dispute over the Lupercalia, Gelasius' opponents accused him of tolerating lax and incompetent priests and of allowing the Church to propagate legends of dubious veracity. In response, Gelasius held a synod in the spring of 494 at which he issued new rules on clerical behaviour and saw that they were enforced. He also ordered the papal bureaucracy to draw up a list of works that should be accepted as genuine Christian tracts, and which should be discarded as being either heretical or of unproven origins. That original list has since been lost and the list known as the Decretum Gelasianum which survives is of a rather later date. In it the Syrian Life is mentioned. It is listed as being of dubious origins, but not condemned outright. Crucially the martyr George is listed among those "whose names are justly reverenced among men, but whose actions are known only to God." In other words, George was accepted as having been a genuine martyr, but the details given in the Syrian Life are dismissed.

Despite Gelasius trying to suppress the more outlandish accounts of the martyrdom of St George, they continued to spread, as did other tales about him. In the 680s a Frankish bishop named Arculf visited Lydda and paid his respects to the shrine of St George. He was rather surprised to see the otherwise humble priest riding about on a magnificent horse. Arculf was told that a rich local merchant had been travelling from Diospolis when he got into trouble. He had offered a quick prayer to St George and promised to donate his horse to the saint if he got home safely. The man had completed his journey without mishap, but had then forgotten all about his promise. That very night St George had appeared at the man's house and put a curse on the horse making it wild and unmanageable. The man had then led the horse to the Church of St George and tied it to the door, whereupon the animal had become docile again. And so, the priest said, he had gained a fine mount.

The popularity of St George continued unabated. Churches to him were founded in London, Windsor and Oxford and many writers included versions of his story in their works.

In 741 the Greek priest Zacharias of Calabria became Pope. He was delighted to find among the various treasures in the papal residence of the Lateran Palace a box inside which he found the preserved head of St George. Zacharias recognised the importance of the sacred relic and had it moved from the dusty storeroom to pride of place in a church of its own. He chose the church of St Sebastian beside the Arch of Janus by the Palatine Hill. The church was rededicated to St George, refurbished and embellished. It is likely that Zacharias chose the church as it served the Greek community of merchants resident in Rome.

Over the following centuries the fame of St George the Martyr spread and increased. In those countries that recognised the Pope in Rome as the head of the Christian Church, George acquired the title of "Saint". He did so along with many other early Christian martyrs as the developing Christian theology produced the concept that outstandingly holy individuals should be recognised as saints. In Greek-

A Dark Age Saint

The gateway to the medieval monastery of St Albans, built on the site of the dark age monastery dedicated to this very British saint. *Gary Houston*

speaking lands he became known as a "megalomartyr", which translates as "great martyr" and indicated that he should be revered more highly than ordinary martyrs.

In the west the concept of a saint was changing. At the time that George lived, it was enough for a Christian to pray to God and to believe that Jesus Christ was His son. By about 600, however, it was coming to be believed that we poor mortals needed a bit of help when talking to the Almighty. That is where saints came in. It was believed that those who had led especially holy lives or who had performed acts — such as martyrdom — that were highly regarded by God occupied a special place in Heaven close to the throne of God. On the other hand, the saints had been humans in life and this gave them rather more empathy with other mortals than was shown by angels,

St Alban was martyred in the Hertfordshire town that now bears his name by being beheaded by the Roman authorities, probably in 283.
Przemyslaw Sakrajda

archangels and other sacred beings. Over the years it became increasingly common practice to address a prayer or request to a saint, effectively asking them to pass it on to God on behalf of the human making the prayer.

The concept was formalised as a result of the Second Council of Nicaea, held in 787. This was the seventh great meeting of all the bishops of Christendom and had been summoned by the Patriarch of Constantinople Paul VI to discuss a variety of issues that were causing debate within Christianity. The Council emphasised that worship was due to God alone, but that prayers could be addressed to saints so long as it was clear the ultimate recipient of the prayer was God and that the saint was merely a messenger. They coined the words "latria" for the worship of God and "dulia" for the veneration of saints. The subtle distinction was lost on most people who took up praying to saints with enthusiasm.

Among the customs that began to grow up around the veneration of saints was the enthusiastic veneration of relics. As early as the 350s there is evidence that Christians believed it would do them good to be buried close to the tomb of a saint. By the 430s the Byzantine theologian Theodoretus was expressing the view that the sanctity of a saint was present in each part of his body, which meant that a saint's skeleton did not need to include very single bone to be a validly sacred relic. Before long many devout Christians were taking this view to mean that any part of a saint's body was as sacred and holy as the whole. As a result saint's bodies began to be divided up and spread about to ensure that the holy power of the saint's body was present in as many places as possible. The division of a saint's skeleton – and other relics such as cups, cloaks and shoes – could happen surprisingly quickly and completely.

One account written in about 570 by Gregory of Tours states that after his death the body of St George was moved from the place of martyrdom in the square of Lydda by a group of local Christians. They were given a room for the night in a local hospital, intending to bury the body next day. When dawn came the burial party found that the door to their room was miraculously wedged shut and that they could not open it. After some discussion they decided that this meant that St George was intervening to stop their journey and that they had to leave a part of his holy body in the hospital as a relic to be venerated. Once they had removed a body part (Gregory does not say which part) the door to their chamber was freed as miraculously as it had been locked and they could get on with the funeral.

It must be said that Gregory of Tours is not generally regarded as the finest of historical scholars. His works tend to pass on any gossip or story that he heard, and he seems to have made no effort at all to have checked up on his sources. The tale of St George's body at the hospital was probably one such tale picked up by a pilgrim to the Holy Land and passed on to Gregory. That a hospital did have a relic of St George and did claim to have acquired it in the way Gregory describes is very likely. Whether the tale is true or not is another matter.

At some date around 743 the villagers of Portbail in Normandy found a large cylindrical casket washed up on the beach. Debris washed up was nothing new, but this casket was clearly expensively made and just as clearly securely locked. The villagers took it to their local priest, who called in higher authorities. When the casket was finally opened it was found to contain a beautifully written and decorated copy of the gospels and a number of relics. One of these relics was the jawbone of St George, complete with a parchment tag giving a detailed account of its provenance and origins.

Count Ricwin of Cotentin had arrived by this point. He declared that the arrival of the casket was a sign of the hand of God. Divine guidance, he said, should now decide where the holy and valuable relics should go next. He loaded the casket and its contents on to a cart pulled by two oxen, gave the oxen a good hard prod to get them moving and followed in their footsteps. The oxen wandered around for some hours before stopping outside the village of Brix. Ricwin promptly donated enough money to build a small church dedicated to St George in which the relics were housed. St George then became rather popular in Normandy, with over two dozen churches being dedicated to him in the next 50 years.

The problems of tracking down the relics of St George can best be illustrated by dealing with his head. As noted above, the head of St George was discovered in a box by Pope Zacharias in the 740s. The head was donated by a later pope to the city of Ferrara, which dedicated its cathedral to St George by way of thanks. The citizens of Lydda, meanwhile, denied that the saint's head had left their own town and claimed it was still buried in their church. That did not stop the people living on Reichenau Island in Lake Constance, Germany, from stating that they had the real head. In the 10th century they went so far as to build a special church to house the relic. In 1453 some monks fleeing Constantinople after it fell to the Ottoman Turks claimed to have carried away the head of St George from the church where it had been resting since having been taken to the imperial city a thousand years earlier. Then in the 1470s King Edward IV of England presented the head of St George – complete with helmet – to St George's Chapel in Windsor Castle. It was displayed in the South Aisle until 1642 when Roundhead troopers broke into the chapel and in an excess of puritanical zeal smashed up all reliquaries and statues. Finally, in 1971, restoration work at St George's Monastery in Venice revealed a medieval reliquary holding a severed skull. Perhaps inevitably this was identified as being that of St George.

The real St George could not possibly have so many heads, so quite how the different heads came to be venerated as his is open to question. Perhaps a head belonged to a local martyr named George and was mistakenly linked to the St George of Lydda later on, or perhaps outright fraud was involved. Whatever the case, the proliferation of heads of St George clearly shows how widespread and firm was the veneration of the saint.

A silver penny of King Edward the Confessor. The king was declared a saint in 1161 and for some years was patron saint of England.

It must be said that although the veneration of St George was widespread throughout Christendom, he was not especially popular. Churches and shrines dedicated to St George were erected in all areas of Europe, North Africa and the Middle East but they were always outnumbered by those sacred to other saints.

The versions of St George's life story that were produced between the time of Pope Gelasius and the 11th century placed increasing emphasis on his courage in the face of torture and death. The details of the tortures endured changed regularly and became increasingly bizarre and painful. He was routinely described as a soldier and whenever a picture of him was drawn or painted it showed him clad in the armour of the period and wielding a spear or sword. Several churchmen wrote books that were either about him or that mentioned him. Although the accounts of St George concentrated on his martyrdom, the fact that he had been a soldier made him a favourite of knights and others going off to war.

It was this fact that was to lead to events in 1098 that were to transform St George forever.

Chapter 3

On Crusade

By the 1080s, the world had changed since George's day. He had lived at the height of the Roman Empire when the Imperial edict had force from northern Britain to the Sahara and from the Atlantic to the Black Sea. The Empire was rich, peaceful and heavily populated. Then had come a change in the climate that devastated crops, causing famines and depopulation. Recurrent economic problems combined with corruption and vested interests to undermine the effectiveness of the Roman government and especially the Roman army. When the barbarians attacked, Rome fell.

At Constantinople, Roman civilisation staggered on in the shape of the Byzantine Empire though it was much reduced in size, wealth and scale. In the west, the Roman Empire was replaced by a selection of kingdoms, duchies and principalities. In 800 the Pope crowned the most powerful of these kings to be Emperor in the west, though the Byzantines disputed the legality of the title and most western kings refused to acknowledge his power.

In the 7th century a new religious and political force exploded on to the scene as the Moslem Arabs surged out of Arabia. The new religion of Islam was spread by the sword across the Middle East and North Africa. Previously Christian lands were taken into the Islamic Caliphate. The conquest was accompanied by the usual massacres, rapes and pillaging, but as occupations go the Islamic occupation of Christian lands was not too onerous. Christians were allowed to continue their religion more or less freely, though they had to pay extra taxes and lacked various legal rights that were enjoyed by Moslem citizens. The temptation to convert to the new religion was strong, and many took the step.

In 996 a new Caliph came to power in the person of Abu Ali Mansur Al Hakim. This Mansur was an especially devout Shiite Moslem who launched a series of persecutions of other religions. Christianity suffered badly, but forms of Islam also came in for hostile treatment. In 1010 soldiers sent by Mansur burned the Church of St George at Lydda that had been built over the saint's tomb by the Emperor Constantine. A priest managed to rescue an arm bone from the ruins and fled north to Constantinople with it. The Emperor had it placed in a reliquary and pledged that one day he would see the church rebuilt and the arm bone replaced in the tomb.

Mansur went on to demolish the Church of the Holy Sepulchre in Jerusalem and to convert various other churches to be mosques. Christians were ordered to wear an iron cross on a leather thong around their necks at all times (Jews had to wear a brass bell), and imposed various Islamic laws on all his subjects. Of particular concern to Christians was the ban on alcohol, since this made it impossible to get wine for use in Holy Communion.

The Byzantine Emperor Basil II objected to this treatment of his fellow Christians, but backed off when Mansur mustered his armies. On 12 February 1021 Mansur set off alone to spend a night fasting and praying in the hills west of Cairo. He vanished and no trace of him was ever found. His son and successor Ali Zahir relaxed some of the anti-Christian laws, but refused to allow any churches to be rebuilt. The tomb of St George was neglected and deteriorated.

In 1071 the Battle of Manzikert saw the Byzantines utterly defeated by a Moslem army. The Emperor Romanos IV was captured and some 30,000 square miles of wealthy agricultural land fell to the Moslems. The huge, wealthy cities of Antioch, Edessa and Hierapolis were also captured. Antioch was so large that its walls were over 18 miles long, and Edessa was not much smaller. Over the following 20 years, the

Byzantine Empire was reduced to half the size it had been before Manzikert. By 1095 the Moslem scouts were almost within sight of Constantinople itself. Emperor Alexios I decided to call on his fellow Christians for help. He sent a message to Pope Urban II asking him to issue an appeal for Christian warriors to come to help him recapture the lost lands.

Urban set out on a series of travels spreading the word that Christianity was under dire threat. His messengers travelled through Europe retelling reports of Moslem brutality to Christians. Knights and soldiers were particularly interested to learn that the shrine of their most revered soldier saint, St George, was among those that had been burnt and that it still lay in ruins. The aim of rebuilding the shrine at Lydda became one of the rallying points for the army that Urban was gathering.

In the late summer of 1096 a huge number of people began arriving in Constantinople from Europe. Many were soldiers, knights and nobles but others were unarmed pilgrims who wanted to add their prayers to the weapons of the fighting men in the effort to overcome the Moslems. By April 1097 an estimated 40,000 fighting men and 20,000 others were in place. They were led by a number of noblemen including Duke Robert of Normandy, Count Raymond of Toulouse, Count Adhemar of Le Puy, Prince Bohemond of Taranto and Godfrey of Bouillon. The force became known as the Crusade — historians call it the First Crusade — from the Latin word crux meaning cross.

Escorted by a large Byzantine army under the general Tatikios, the Crusaders marched into Anatolia to capture Nicaea. They then pushed on toward Jerusalem. On the march a clear difference of purpose emerged. The crusaders wanted to capture Jerusalem, rebuild the ruined churches and make the area once again safe for Christian pilgrims and residents. Tatikios wanted to return the lost lands to Byzantine control. Both objectives involved defeating the Moslem armies, so the two Christian forces cooperated. At Antioch, the dispute came into the open.

The Crusaders wanted to capture the great city of Antioch to act as

The charge of the Christian knights, inspired by a vision of St George,
led by Duke Robert of Normandy at the Battle of Antioch
during the First Crusade.

a port through which supplies and reinforcements could reach them
from Europe. They would then march south to Jerusalem. Tatikios
wanted to ignore Antioch and march north to defeat the Seljuq Turks.
As the siege of Antioch dragged on, Tatikios lost patience and led his
army north. He left the Crusaders with some help, however. The
reliquary holding the arm bone of St George was left with the
Crusaders in the hope that they could return it to Lydda.

After eight months of siege, Antioch fell when a Christian soldier within opened the gates to his fellow Christians. The Crusaders robbed the local Moslems, killing any who resisted, but then found themselves in serious trouble. No sooner were they in the city than a huge Moslem army led by Kerbogha of Mosul arrived. Kerbogha had aimed to defeat the Crusaders and lift the siege, but now he laid siege to the city instead. His army outnumbered the Christians and was well fed, while the Christians were short on food and water. One of the poor pilgrims named Peter Bartholomew then had a vision that led him to uncover a spear that he declared to be the Holy Lance that had pierced Christ's side as He hung on the cross.

On 25 June the Crusaders began three solid days of prayers and religious processions, moving from one church in Antioch to the next in an endless round of devotions. At dawn on 28 June they marched out of the city to do battle with Kerbogha and his host. Bohemond led the way with his personal troops, while Adhemar, Godfry and Raymond led other sections. Robert of Normandy was there, so was an English prince named Edgar. Only 100 knights had horses fit for battle so most of the Christians fought on foot. The army was followed by a host of pilgrims in simple tunics and walking barefoot shouting prayers. Among them was Peter and the Holy Lance. Battle was joined and the killing began. One force of Moslems sought to ride around the flank of the Crusaders to get to the open gates of Antioch, but Bohemond led a force of knights to block the move.

Then the Christians saw a remarkable thing. A lone horseman wearing armour and a white cloak appeared on a hill behind the Moslem army. Another horseman joined the first, this man carrying a white banner very different from the green and black flags of Kerbogha's men. Soon a small knot of armoured horsemen was gathered on the hilltop. A force of cavalry detached itself from the Moslem army and spurred toward the new arrivals. As the Moslem men rode up the slope, the man in white lifted his sword high over his head. The white banner was waved three times, then the horsemen surged down the slope in a disciplined charge. The Moslem horsemen turned tail and fled without striking a blow. The fleeing men rode across the rear of Kerbogha's army shouting, screaming and pointing in fear at the advancing men under the white banner. Within minutes the vast Moslem army broke up and fled. The Crusaders had won a great victory.

Strangely there was no sign of the man in white nor the men who had ridden into battle under the white banner. The riders who had caused the Moslems to break and run had vanished. For the Crusaders there was only one possible explanation. They had been holy warriors sent by God. And their leader could have been nobody but St George, the soldier saint. Soon men were saying that the white banner had been emblazoned with a red cross.

It was a miracle.

The veneration of St George was transformed by the Battle of Antioch. Up until this point the emblem of a red cross on a white field had been widely used as a symbol of Christian martyrdom. The cross symbolised faith in Christ, the red stood for the blood of the martyr while the white indicated purity of faith. The Crusaders now identified the symbol with St George. It was to be many years before the red cross on a white field became the exclusive property of St George as many traditionalists continued to use it as a generic symbol of martyrs, but the process proved to be inexorable.

And while St George had long been a soldier saint, he was now very much a fighting saint. He had drawn his sword in battle against the Moslems and caused their destruction. Pictures of him began to show him in belligerent mood. No longer was he shown standing passively in armour, he was now shown riding a prancing horse, waving a sword or lance as if going into battle and sometimes he was depicted actively slaughtering Moslems by the dozen.

The Crusaders stayed at Antioch for some time while reinforcements arrived and the supply system was sorted out. Then they swept on toward Jerusalem. They were helped by the fact that the caliphate that had unified the Moslem rulers had collapsed. The Christians were faced in the Holy Land by a number of small, feuding Moslem states none of which could field a particularly large army.

Having secured victory at Antioch following a vision of St George, the crusaders were similarly inspired by St George during the assault on the walls of Jerusalem.

At Lydda, the Crusaders paused at the ruins of the Church of St George. The arm bone was returned to the broken tomb and rebuilding work began. The Crusaders rebuilt the Church of St George as befitted their new warrior saint. The new structure was larger than the old one had been. It was stoutly built of stone, equipped with battlements and provided with a tower as big and strong as a castle keep. The new Church of St George was an impressive stronghold.

Construction work was still in hand as the Crusaders swept on to their ultimate prize: Jerusalem. The governor of the city, Iftikhar ad-Daula had expelled all Christians from the city, not wanting to see one of his gates opened as at Antioch. A siege began on 7 June 1099. By 8 July the Christians had completed their siege towers, had battered the walls with catapults and were ready to attack. The entire army then prayed and fasted for two days, after which they processed barefoot around the city walls singing hymns.

The attack began at dawn on 14 July, and raged throughout the day and into the night. Stones and flaming bales of hay were hurled into the city to set fire to houses, while boulders pummelled the walls. The defenders shot back with arrows, stones and flaming pitch. Several of the Crusaders towers and catapults were destroyed by rocks hurled from the walls. Just before dawn the Christian commanders met to discuss the situation. Their men had been attacking in relays so that fresh men replaced those tired by fighting. Soon all the men would have served two terms in the front line and could not be asked for more.

As the cold grey light of a new day spread over the fighting, a great cry went up from a group of Crusaders. A knight dressed all in white and carrying a white banner could be seen standing on the Mount of Olives. This was the spot from which Jesus Christ had ascended into Heaven, according to the Bible, and had special significance for the Crusaders. Obviously the knight was St George, come back again to work his miraculous help for the Crusaders. The knight in white waved his banner forwards, pointing toward the siege tower manned by the Flemish contingent. Two knights, Litold and Gilbert, hurled themselves from the tower on to the walls of the city. They cut down the defenders, then hauled up other Christians to join them. Soon the Flemings had a secure foothold, allowing dozens of others to clamber up to join them. Then the Moslems fled, seeking the shelter of the impregnable Tower of David. The Crusaders were into Jerusalem, pillaging and killing at will.

St George had worked yet another military miracle.

Next day, Iftikhar ad-Daula and the men who had joined him in the Tower of David were allowed to march out of the city. The civilians who had survived the night of pillage were also allowed to leave, though they had to leave behind everything of any value.

The Kingdom of Jerusalem that the Crusaders had founded stretched from Edessa in the north, through Antioch, Tripoli, Acre and Jerusalem to embrace both shores of the Dead Sea and reach as far south as the Red Sea. For almost one hundred years the Kingdom of Jerusalem kept open the pilgrim routes for Christians from Europe heading for Nazareth, Jerusalem and Bethlehem. The Church of St George at Lydda was a favoured stopping point for knights on the road from the coast to Jerusalem.

Then a new Moslem ruler managed to unite all the Islamic states in the Middle East under his personal control. Salah ad-Din, known to Christians as Saladin, believed it to be his sacred duty to drive the Christians out of what had once been Moslem lands. In 1187 at the

The triumph of Saladin at the Battle of the Horns of Hattin in 1187 transformed the military situation in the Holy Land. The Crusaders lost Jerusalem and dozens of other towns and castles.

Battle of Hattin he almost wiped out the army of the Kingdom of Jerusalem, and captured King Guy. Saladin's troops fanned out to ride across the Kingdom of Jerusalem, capturing castles and towns denuded of their troops and left leaderless by the losses at Hattin.

At Lydda, the entire Christian population locked themselves up in the Church of St George. Saladin's men could do nothing against the strong defences of the church, and with Jerusalem beckoning did not have time for a siege. The Christians of Lydda negotiated their way to safety. Jerusalem fell after an heroic siege, followed by the main crusader strongholds and cities. Soon only Tyre, Antioch and a few coastal castles remained in Christian hands.

The disaster of Hattin and the fall of Jerusalem echoed through Christendom. King Richard I of England, better known as Richard the Lionheart, King Philip II of France and many others vowed to set off for the Holy Land to defeat Saladin. Philip arrived first in April and laid siege to the great port city of Acre. He was joined by Duke Leopold of Austria, Duke Frederick of Swabia and others, but they failed to make any impression of the formidable walls. On 8 June 1191, Richard the Lionheart arrived with the English crusaders. His first act was typical of his headstrong and tactless character, and could have led to a disastrous dispute with the French. A large supply ship with pigs crated on deck was sighted off the coast flying the flag of France. Richard's men were short on food, so Richard ordered that the French ship be stopped and forced to sell some food to the English. Once the ship was boarded, it was found to be a Moslem ship heading to relieve Acre. The ship was captured, the stores seized and Richard was triumphant.

Using the incident with the ship as an example, of his superior warlike gifts, Richard began issuing orders and insisting that the siege had to be done according to his methods. Richard was a famously competent soldier and was deeply unimpressed by the efforts being made by his Christian allies. Undoubtedly Richard was right to set the men to build catapults and siege engines to his preferred design, but it was tactless. After all, the Christians had been besieging Acre for almost two years and Richard had only just arrived.

The work was almost complete when Richard fell ill with a fever that caused some of his hair to fall out. Richard was confined to his bed as he slipped in and out of consciousnesses. While he was ill a breach was opened in the city walls. The Christians marched to attack, but the Moslem defenders set up a great shout and banged their drums. This alerted a small army under Saladin that was hiding in nearby hills. Saladin swept down to attack the Christian camp, forcing the Crusaders to call off the attack. By the time order was restored, the defenders had patched up repairs to their wall.

On 10 July Richard suddenly recovered. He sprang from his bed declaring that he had had a vision. Summoning his commanders, Richard told them that St George had appeared to him while he had been helpless with fever and told him to attack Acre at once. While Richard had been ill, the new siege engines had indeed battered a hole in the walls, so next day the Crusaders attacked. They were driven off but the fighting had been so severe that the defenders surrendered next day.

Baha al-Din Qaragush, who commanded at Acre, agreed to a huge ransom of 200,000 gold coins, the release of 1,500 Christians held as slaves by Saladin and the return of the True Cross that had been lost to Saladin at Hattin. Saladin tried to renegotiate the terms, stating they were too extreme, but Richard refused. When Saladin was late with an installment of the ransom, Richard declared that the Moslems had broken the terms of the surrender. He ordered his men to execute the captured garrison, sending 2,700 men to their deaths. Saladin responded by killing all his prisoners as well. The war entered a new and more murderous phase.

For the next year Richard rampaged through the Holy Land, beating the Moslems time and again but never inflicting a decisive defeat on Saladin. At one point he visited Lydda to pray at the tomb of St George. Finding the church in a poor state of disrepair, Richard donated money to rebuild the church. With this money, and other gifts from crusaders, the church was rebuilt. The church was made the cathedral of a Bishop of Lydda, who performed services according to

King Richard the Lionheart of England leads a charge of Christian knights during the Third Crusade. It was a vision of St George by King Richard that boosted St George's fame in England.

the western tradition and owed his allegiance to the Pope.

Finally, Richard and Saladin negotiated a peace that left Jerusalem in Moslem hands, but kept it open to Christian pilgrims, while the newly appointed King Henry of Jerusalem gained enough lands and castles to make the Christian grip on parts of the Holy Land secure for another century. The Christians would finally be driven out of the Holy Land in 1291. The "Kingdom of Jerusalem" was then restricted to the island of Cyprus, which finally fell to the Turks in 1570.

The Bishop of Lydda was driven from his cathedral and the see lapsed into inactivity in the 1260s. The church remained and was used by those Christians who still lived in the area, but it once again fell into disrepair. In about 1450 the church was rebuilt, but again fell into neglect. By 1800 only the outer walls remained.

King Richard's vision at Acre was the last time that St George intervened in the crusades. But he was far from idle. There was the little matter of a ferocious dragon to deal with.

Chapter 4

Enter The Dragon

Exactly when the dragon first entered the story of St George is a matter of some dispute. The first written account of St George fighting a dragon does not appear until the 1240s, by which time St George was rapidly gaining in fame as a result of his exploits in the crusades. However, icons of him produced in the Byzantine Empire had been showing him fighting a dragon since at least the 800s. As we have already seen a snake or serpent may well have been present in some form inside the original Church of St George in Lydda from the 330s.

The dragon in Byzantine icons is usually symbolic of pagans or paganism. Angels and saints are often shown trampling on dead or humbled dragons to symbolise the pure faith of the Christian figure triumphing over paganism. St George is more often shown fighting the dragon than trampling on it, presumably because he was known to be a soldier saint.

However St George got linked to the dragon, it is certain that icons painted in the Byzantine Empire were showing him triumphing over a dragon by the time the Crusaders took up the veneration of the saint in a big way after the siege of Antioch. Several of those crusaders brought back to western Europe souvenirs of their time in the East when they returned home. Among these are known to have been icons of the saints, St George among them. None of those icons taken to western Europe have survived, but it is reasonable to assume that at least some of those showing St George also showed a dragon.

Some of these icons were brought back to Europe, and were copied locally. Two early copies exist in English churches. At Brinsop in Herefordshire there is a carving of St George riding a horse and spearing a dragon with his lance. The carving dates to around 1160 or so. Rather earlier is the carving in St George's Church in Fordington, Dorset. This shows the saint in a similar pose, but this time he is spearing human soldiers instead of a dragon. It is presumed that this carving shows the Battle of Antioch.

The fame of St George and the Dragon was widespread in England. At Uffington in Berkshire there is a complex of prehistoric monuments including a hillfort, long barrow, white horse and standing stones. At the foot of the towering 850 foot hill on which these monuments stand there is a small, isolated hillock that goes by the name of Dragon Hill. The top of the hillock is made of bare chalk where nothing will grow. Local legend has it that the chalk remains bare because when St George killed the dragon here, the dragon's blood flooded out to poison the ground for all eternity.

Some time around the year 1230 or so one of the icons of St George brought back to Europe by crusaders came into the hands of a Dominican friar named Vincent of Beauvais. Vincent was engaged on producing one of the longest books ever written, the Speculum Maius, or Great Mirror. This vast book is a form of encyclopedia that ran to something over 8,000 chapters and included information on subjects as diverse as military tactics, life cycles of birds, the causes of rain and how to perform religious rituals.

Buried in the Speculum Maius is a shortened version of the Syrian Life of St George with its tale of martyrdom at the hands of the pagan governor Dadianos. Vincent inserted into the story a brief reference to a battle with a dragon, presumably to explain the presence of the dragon on the icon that he had.

Thirty years later, in about 1260, another writer elaborated on the dragon motif and created the basic legend of St George and the Dragon that is repeated today.

Jacobus de Voragine was an Italian priest who would later rise to

Dragon Hill in Berkshire. According to a local legend St George
killed the dragon here and the serpent s blood poisoned the
ground so nothing can grow here.

become Archbishop of Genoa. In 1260, however, he was Prior of the
Dominican Priory at Bologna and had time on his hands. He decided
to fill his time by collecting together biographies of all the more
important saints of his time. He called his book the Legenda Sanctorum,
or Readings of the Saints, but it became better known as the Legenda
Aurea, or Golden Legend. The book was an instant success with
hundreds of copies being made by hand within a few years of its

compilation. It would later become a bestseller in the early days of printing — at one point outselling the Bible itself.

The Golden Legend drew on a variety of sources for its many tales and anecdotes. So far over a hundred likely originals for the material in the book have been identified and it is generally thought that Voragine based his chapter on St George on the book by Vincent. However, Voragine included a much longer and more elaborate version of St George's battle with the dragon than had Vincent. Where this story came from, nobody has ever been able to prove. Perhaps Voragine simply made it up.

The story as told by Voragine goes like this:

Of Saint George, Martyr, and first the interpretation of his name.

George is said of "geos", which is as much to say as "earth", and "orge" that is "tilling". So George is to say as tilling the earth, that is his flesh. And Saint Austin saith, in libro de Trinitate that, good earth is in the height of the mountains, in the temperance of the valleys, and in the plain of the fields. The first is good for herbs being green, the second to vines, and the third to wheat and corn. Thus the blessed George was high in despising low things, and therefore he had verdure in himself, he was attemperate by discretion, and therefore he had wine of gladness, and within he was plane of humility, and thereby put he forth wheat of good works. Or George may be said of "gerar", that is "holy", and of "gyon", that is a "wrestler", that is an holy wrestler, for he wrestled with the dragon. Or George is said of "gero", that is a pilgrim, and "gir", that is detrenched out, and "ys", that is a councillor. He was a pilgrim in the sight of the world, and he was cut and detrenched by the crown of martyrdom, and he was a good councillor in preaching.

And his legend is numbered among other scriptures apocryphal in the council of Nicene, because his martyrdom hath no certain relation. For in the calendar of Bede it is said that he suffered martyrdom in Persia in the city of Diaspolin, and in other places it is read that he resteth in the city of Diaspolin which tofore was called Lidda, which is by the city of Joppa or Japh. And in another place it is said that he suffered death under Diocletian and Maximian, which at that time were emperors. And in another place under Diocletian emperor of Persia, being present seventy kings of his empire. And it is said here that he suffered death under Dacian the provost, then Diocletian and Maximian being emperors.

Here followeth the Life of Saint George martyr.

Saint George was a knight and born in Cappadocia. On a time he came in to the province of Libya, to a city which is said Silene. And by this city was a stagne or a pond like a sea, wherein was a dragon which envenomed all the country. And on a time the people were assembled for to slay him, and when they saw him they fled. And when he came nigh the city he venomed the people with his breath, and therefore the people of the city gave to him every day two sheep for to feed him, because he should do no harm to the people, and when the sheep failed there was taken a man and a sheep. Then was an ordinance made in the town that there should be taken the children and young people of them of the town by lot, and every each one as it fell, were he gentle or poor, should be delivered when the lot fell on him or her.

So it happed that many of them of the town were then delivered, insomuch that the lot fell upon the king's daughter, whereof the king was sorry, and said unto the people: "For the love of the gods take gold and silver and all that I have, and let me have my daughter." They said: "How sir! ye have made and ordained the law, and our children be now dead, and ye would do the contrary. Your daughter shall be given, or else we shall burn you and your house."

When the king saw he might no more do, he began to weep, and said to his daughter: "Now shall I never see thine espousals." Then returned he to the people and demanded eight days' respite, and they granted it to him. And when the eight days were passed they came to him and said: "Thou seest that the city perisheth": Then did the king do array his daughter like as she should be wedded, and embraced her, kissed her and gave her his benediction, and after, led her to the place where the dragon was.

The image of St George over the entrance to his tomb in Lod shows him slaying a dragon. This relief was carved in 1897 when the church was restored. *Haltiamieli*

When she was there Saint George passed by, and when he saw the lady he demanded the lady what she made there and she said: "Go ye your way fair young man, that ye perish not also." Then said he: "Tell to me what have ye and why weep ye, and doubt ye of nothing." When she saw that he would know, she said to him how she was delivered to the dragon. Then said Saint George: "Fair daughter, doubt ye no thing hereof for I shall help thee in the name of Jesu Christ." She said: "For God's sake, good knight, go your way, and abide not with me, for ye may not deliver me."

Thus as they spake together the dragon appeared and came running to them, and Saint George was upon his horse, and drew out his sword and garnished him with the sign of the cross, and rode hardily against the dragon which came towards him, and smote him with his spear and hurt him sore and threw him to the ground. And after said to the maid: "Deliver to me your girdle, and bind it about the neck of the dragon and be not afeard." When she had done so the dragon followed her as it had been a meek beast and debonair. Then she led him into the city, and the people fled by mountains and valleys, and said: "Alas! Alas! We shall be all dead." Then Saint George said to them: "Ne doubt ye no thing, without more, believe ye in God, Jesu Christ, and do ye to be baptized and I shall slay the dragon."

Then the king was baptized and all his people, and Saint George slew the dragon and smote off his head, and commanded that he should be thrown in the fields, and they took four carts with oxen that drew him out of the city.

Then were there well fifteen thousand men baptized, without women and children, and the king did do make a church there of our Lady and of Saint George, in the which yet sourdeth a fountain of living

A 12th century relief from the Church of St George in Fordington, Dorset, shows the saint slaughtering Moslem soldiers while Christian knights kneel in prayer.

water, which healeth sick people that drink thereof. After this the king offered to Saint George as much money as there might be numbered, but he refused all and commanded that it should be given to poor people for God's sake; and enjoined the king four things, that is, that he should have charge of the churches, and that he should honour the priests and hear their service diligently, and that he should have pity on the poor people, and after, kissed the king and departed.

Now it happed that in the time of Diocletian and Maximian, which were emperors, was so great persecution of christian men that within a month were martyred well twenty-two thousand, and therefore they had so great dread that some reneged and forsook God and did sacrifice to the idols. When Saint George saw this, he left the habit of a knight and sold all that he had, and gave it to the poor, and took the habit of a christian man, and went into the middle of the pagans and began to cry: "All the gods of the pagans be devils, my God made the heavens and is very God." Then said the provost to him: "Of what presumption cometh this to thee, that thou sayest that our gods be devils? And say to us what thou art and what is thy name." He answered anon and said: "I am named George, I am a gentleman, a knight of Cappadocia, and have left all for to serve the God of heaven."

Then the provost enforced himself to draw him unto his faith by fair words, and when he might not bring him thereto he did do raise him on a gibbet; and so much beat him with great staves and broches of iron, that his body was all to broken in pieces. And after he did do take brands of iron and join them to his sides, and his bowels which then appeared he did do frot with salt, and so sent him into prison, but our Lord appeared to him the of same night with great light and comforted him much sweetly. And by this great consolation he took to him so good heart that he feared no torment that they might make him suffer.

Then, when Dacian the provost saw that he might not surmount him, he called his enchanter and said to him: "I see that these christian people fear not our torments." The enchanter bound himself, upon his head to be smitten off, if he overcame not his crafts. Then he did take strong venom and meddled it with wine, and made invocation of the names of his false gods, and gave it to Saint George to drink. Saint George took it and made the sign of the cross on it, and anon drank it without grieving him any thing. Then the enchanter made it more stronger than it was tofore of venom, and gave it him to drink, and it grieved him nothing. When the enchanter saw that, he kneeled down at the feet of Saint George and prayed him that he would make him christian. And when Dacian knew that he was become christian he made to smite off his head.

And after, on the morn, he made Saint George to be set between two wheels, which were full of swords, sharp and cutting on both sides, but anon the wheels were broken and Saint George escaped without hurt. And then commanded Dacian that they should put him in a caldron full of molten lead, and when Saint George entered therein, by the virtue of our Lord it seemed that he was in a bath well at ease. Then Dacian seeing this began to assuage his ire, and to flatter him by fair words, and said to him: "George, the patience of our gods is over great unto thee which hast blasphemed them, and done to them great despite, then fair, and right sweet son, I pray thee that thou return to our law and make sacrifice to the idols, and leave thy folly, and I shall enhance thee to great honour and worship." Then began Saint George to smile, and said to him: Wherefore saidst thou not to me thus at the beginning? I am ready to do as thou sayest. Then was Dacian glad and made to cry over all the town that all the people should assemble for to see George make sacrifice which so much had striven there against. Then was the city arrayed and feast kept throughout all the town, and all came to the temple for to see him.

When Saint George was on his knees, and they supposed that he would have worshipped the idols, he prayed our Lord God of heaven that he would destroy the temple and the idol in the honour of his name, for to make the people to be converted. And anon the fire descended from heaven and burnt the temple, and the idols, and their priests, and sith the earth opened and swallowed all the cinders and ashes that were left. Then Dacian made him to be brought tofore him, and said to him: "What be the evil deeds that thou hast done and also great untruth?" Then said to him Saint George: "Ah, sir, believe it not, but come with me and see how I shall sacrifice." Then said Dacian to him: "I see well thy fraud and thy barat, thou wilt make the earth to swallow me, like as thou hast the temple and my gods." Then said Saint George: "O caitiff, tell me how may thy gods help thee when they may not help themselves!"

Then was Dacian so angry that he said to his wife: "I shall die for anger if I may not surmount and overcome this man." Then said she to him: "Evil and cruel tyrant! Now seest thou not the great virtue of the christian people? I said to thee well that thou shouldst not do to them any harm, for their God fighteth for them, and know thou well that I will become christian." Then was Dacian much abashed and said to her: "Wilt thou be christian?" Then he took her by the hair, and did do beat her cruelly. Then demanded she of Saint George: "What may I become because I am not christened?" Then answered the blessed George: "Doubt thee nothing, fair daughter, for thou shalt be baptized in thy blood." Then began she to worship our Lord Jesu Christ, and so she died and went to heaven.

On the morn Dacian gave his sentence that Saint George should be drawn through all the city, and after, his head should be smitten off. Then made he his prayer to our Lord that all they that desired any boon might get it of our Lord God in his name, and a voice came from heaven which said that it which he had desired was granted; and after he had made his orison his head was smitten off, about the year of our Lord two hundred and eighty-seven.

When Dacian went homeward from the place where he was beheaded towards his palace, fire fell down from heaven upon him and burnt him and all his servants.

Gregory of Tours telleth that there were some that bare certain relics of Saint George, and came into a certain oratory in a hospital, and on the morning when they should depart they could not move the door till they had left there part of their relics. It is also found in the history

Painted about 1470 by Italian artist, Paolo Uccello, this picture
shows most elements of the legend of St George as it existed
in the later Middle Ages.

*of Antioch, that when the christian men went over sea to conquer
Jerusalem, that one, a right fair young man, appeared to a priest of
the host and counselled him that he should bear with him a little of the
relics of Saint George. For he was conductor of the battle, and so he
did so much that he had some. And when it was so that they had
assieged Jerusalem and durst not mount nor go up on the walls for the
quarrels and defence of the Saracens, they saw apperatly Saint George
which had white arms with a red cross, that went up tofore them on
the walls, and they followed him, and so was Jerusalem taken by his
help. And between Jerusalem and port Jaffa, by a town called Ramys,
is a chapel of Saint George which is now desolate and uncovered,
and therein dwell christian Greeks. And in the said chapel lieth the
body of Saint George, but not the head. And there lie his father and
mother and his uncle, not in the chapel but under the wall of the
chapel; and the keepers will not suffer pilgrims to come therein, but if
they pay two ducats, and therefore come but few therein, but offer
without the chapel at an altar. And there is seven years and seven lents*

of pardon; and the body of Saint George lieth in the middle of the quire or choir of the said chapel, and in his tomb is an hole that a man may put in his hand. And when a Saracen, being mad, is brought thither, and if he put his head in the hole he shall anon be made perfectly whole, and have his wit again.

There are some points that are worth noting. First, and in common with most medieval writers, Voragine explains matters in terms that would be familiar to his audience. So he describes George as being a "knight" to explain that he was a military man from a wealthy family. The equipment used in the battle by George and the defences of the city are described in detail and are quite clearly of the mid 13th century rather than of Roman type.

Second, the Gregory of Tours who Voragine quotes as a source for a miracle worked by the relics of St George was Bishop of Tours, now in France, from about 573 to his death in about 593. Gregory wrote a history of the Franks, the Germanic tribe that had occupied the former Roman provinces of Gaul at this time. Gregory also wrote a number of theological books and an assortment of books about saints and martyrs. He does not seem to have been very diligent in his researches into miracles ascribed to saints, so it would not be sensible to place too much trust in this account of a miracle performed by St George's relics. What is clear, however, is that as early as the later 6th century George was a saint who was known and talked about as far from the Holy Land as Gaul.

A third point about Voragine's version of the story is that the city of Silenus was an imaginary place. It was, however, named after a minor pagan Greek deity who was a notorious drunk, but who had the gift of prophecy. Voragine was an educated man and although he was writing primarily for a lay audience, he seems to have enjoyed word play and in-jokes aimed at his more educated readership. No doubt his choice of name for this imaginary city was one such.

Moreover, the placing of the incident in Libya shows that the writer wanted to put the dragon in a far away place about which little was known. At this date, "Libya" might have meant almost anywhere in

North Africa. The area was firmly in the hands of Moslem rulers who were hostile to Christendom. Nobody from Europe went there, other than as slaves captured by Moslem raiders. A writer wanting to place a fantastic tale somewhere remote would choose Libya, much as today we would start such a story "Once upon a time..."

The fact that the King dedicates his new church to the Virgin Mary is again a pointer to this tale originating in the 13th century. For the first thousand or so years of its existence, Christianity did not pay much attention to the mother of Christ. From around 1070 the clerics Anselm of Canterbury and Bernard of Clairvaux began to develop a new concept of Mary as an emotional intercessor between humans and her son, Christ. The idea was relatively slow to catch on, but gradually priests found that the softer, more feminine role ascribed to Mary was proving very popular with their flock. By the 1220s the Biblical figure who for generations had been simply "Mary" had become "The Blessed Virgin Mary" and was a major figure in both worship and in theology. Any nobleman wishing to prove himself to be both devout and up to date with the latest trends would make a dedication to the Virgin Mary.

Finally the interests of Voragine as a Dominican friar are reflected in the parting advice given by George to the king. The first three admonitions relate to the king's duties to the organised church, while his charitable works get relegated to fourth place.

In Voragine's version of his martydom, George undergoes the same tortures as specified in the Libyan Life, though Voragine adds a few painful refinements of his own. The pagan tyrant is named as Dacian, not Dadianos, in the Golden Legend and Voragine added a final twist to the story. Perhaps because he could not bear to have Dacian get away with the murder of a dragon-slaying saint, Voragine describes how Dacian walks home after the brutal tortures and execution only to be struck by lightning and consumed by fire raining from heaven.

There is one clue that Voragine may have been working from some older source that he adapts to his own purpose. The story makes great play of the fact that the princess is young, beautiful and rich. Indeed, it seems that it is her physical beauty that first attracts the attention of the passing George. Meanwhile, her father the king spends some time bemoaning the fact that he will never see his daughter married, nor have any grandchildren. Everything seems to be leading up to a happy ending in which George marries the princess, settles down and has children who inherit the kingdom. This never happens, and George simply rides away. As a celibate cleric, Voragine would have had no interest in a love story and may have shared the anti-woman views of many of his contemporary clergymen.

One story that has been suggested as an original source for the version of George's encounter with the dragon in the Golden Legend is the ancient Greek myth of Perseus. In the story, Perseus is the son of the great god Zeus by Danae, daughter of King Acrisius of Argos. Perseus grew up in the household of King Polydectes who wished to marry Danae, though Perseus was opposed to the match. Polydectes therefore sent young Perseus off on a series of apparently impossible errands to keep him out of the way, but Perseus managed to achieve all the tasks set for him with the help of his divine relatives.

On returning from one such errand, Perseus is travelling through Ethiopia when he happens to spot a beautiful princess chained to a rock overlooking the sea. Perseus asks the princess why she is chained up, but she tells him to go away before the sea monster arrives and devours them both. It transpires that the girl is Princess Andromeda whose mother, Queen Cassiopeia, had boasted that she was as beautiful as the Nereids, the divine nymphs of Poseidon, God of the Sea.

Poseidon had taken umbrage at this and sent a sea monster to ravage the lands of Cassiopeia. The monster, Cetus, arrives at Ethiopia and emerges from the sea once each day to devour livestock. An oracle tells Cassiopeia that the monster will continue its activities until Andromeda is offered to it by being chained to a rock by the sea. Hearing the story, Perseus decides to save the beautiful princess.

Perseus battles with the monster Cetus using weapons given him by the gods and kills it. He then releases Andromeda from the rock and returns her to her native city. Perseus then marries Andromeda. After a series of further adventures, Perseus and Andromeda become King and Queen of Mycenae where they have a long and happy reign, establishing a dynasty that ruled the city state for generations.

Although Perseus was a pagan semi-deity, his story was fairly widely known in medieval Europe. Almost certainly Voragine would have known it. The central section in which Perseus rescues a princess from a monster that emerges from the waters is so similar to that of George and the Dragon in the Golden Legend that it seems very likely that Voragine simply adapted the older story, changing it to suit his purposes.

That does not solve the central problem of why Voragine felt the need to add a story about a dragon to what were then the generally accepted facts about St George. True he wanted to produce exciting tales to ensure the popularity of his book among the laity — and so get his moralising messages across to them — but why a dragon with St George? The answer is to be found in ancient Greek mythology. It will be remembered that George was martyred as a consequence of a quarrel with the worshippers of the god Apollo. One of the key symbols of Apollo in ancient Greek art was the snake-deity Python, who Apollo killed as a part of his long-running feud with his stepmother, the goddess Hera. Python was often included in paintings and statues of Apollo to emphasise his fighting skills, and was often worked into the decoration of his temples. Since the old church of St George at Lydda had originally been a temple of Apollo it very likely had snakes carved into its fabric. It is very likely that St George had already become associated with a snake before Voragine began writing. In any case, the serpent was an established symbol of pagan evil by the 13th century. It seems that it was this link to the Python of Apollo that prompted Voragine to include such a monster in his tale of St George.

The popularity of the Golden Legend was enormous, and the tale of St George and the Dragon was one of the best known episodes within it. The veneration of St George was already popular among knights and soldiers, but now his derring do on behalf of winsome young maidens made him popular with ladies as well. Before long, George was popular across the social spectrum. The anniversary of his martyrdom, 23 April, was declared to be a feast day in the 1220s and a double feast in 1415. He was venerated right across Christendom, with churches, chapels and organisations all being dedicated to him.

To this day, St George remains honoured in widely separated areas. He is the patron saint of cities as diverse as Moscow, Genoa and Beirut. He is highly revered in Georgia, which has a variant on the St George's cross on their flag. In India there are more than a dozen shrines to St George in Kerala that date back to the earliest days of Christianity in India. In Ethiopia an entire church of St George has been hacked out of the living rock to form an exotic cave-church of unique design.

But it was in England that St George was to find his home.

A painting of the Crucifixion with Jacobus de Voragine looking on from the left dressed in his robes as Archbishop of Genoa. In his hands he holds a copy of his most famous book.

Chapter 5

A Very English Saint

Today, George is associated more with England than with anywhere else, though he never set foot in the chill northern kingdom. Nevertheless, the first appearance of St George in England came early, in about 700, and he has never really left.

The Northumbrian monk and historian, Bede, wrote a number of works that have survived to the present day and was reckoned to be one of the best educated men in Europe. Among his many works was a Martyrology in which he listed all the martyrs that were known to him. Among them was St George of Lydda who, Bede writes, was martyred by a pagan king of Persia named Datian on 23 April. Bede stated that the tomb of St George lay in Lydda.

Meanwhile, the saint was slowly becoming better known in England. In about 997 Abbot Aelfric of Eynsham produced a series of Lives of Saints which he wrote in English verse. His aim was that the poetic works should be read out to lay audiences to pass away the long winter evenings. Aelfric was worried that it was only clergy and monks who were learning about holy saints and martyrs and they, Aelfric thought, did not really need to dwell on the examples set by such men. The laity, however, would profit from hearing about fine examples of how to lead good Christian lives instead of listening to heroic tales of warriors and singing bawdy songs.

St George was among the saints whose lives Aelfric turned into long poems for public recitals. He rendered the story of St George's martyrdom into everyday English, and his book proved to be surprisingly popular. Among the lay men who heard Aelfric's story being read out was King Canute, more properly Cnut. Canute had been born a pagan Danish prince, but converted to Christianity when he looked likely to inherit the English throne. His Christianity was never much more than skin deep (he kept both his wives for a start) but he proved to be a generous patron of the established Church. In the 1020s he founded a monastery at Thetford that was dedicated to St George, and gave it generous endowments of land.

At about the same time a Church of St George was built in Southwark, though we do not know what role, if any, Canute had in this. Other churches of St George existed at Windsor and Oxford. Once news of the saint's appearances at Antioch and Jerusalem came back to England, other churches were built or rededicated in his honour. He also appears in carvings and paintings.

In 1120 St George at Antioch was painted on the walls of St Botolph's Church at Harham, Sussex. At Damerham in Hampshire a carving of about the same date shows St George slaughtering the Moslems at Antioch. He is shown mounted on a warhorse and dressed as a contemporary knight.

At Clun in Shropshire, near the Welsh Marches, a new church was built and dedicated to St George. Just like the contemporary church of St George in Lydda, the structure at Clun was as much a small fortress as it was a large church. A chapel of St George, now lost, was erected at Shrewsbury, again near Wales. Presumably his warlike exploits made St George a suitable saint for a warlike area. Such dedications were not, however, out of the ordinary as similar features of St George were cropping up across Christendom as his fame spread.

At this date, England already had two patron saints and nobody thought that there was a vacancy for a third. The oldest of the two English saints was St Edmund the Martyr, who had been a King of the East Angles when East Anglia had been an independent kingdom. He came from the ancient Wuffing dynasty that could trace its ancestry back to the 3rd century. Although the earliest Wuffing kings had claimed to be descended from the pagan god Woden, Edmund was a devout Christian who delayed his coronation by some months so that it could take place on Christmas Day 855.

It is difficult not to feel sorry for Edmund. He led a blameless life, ruled his lands well and remained at peace with his fellow kings — only for his kingdom to be suddenly invaded by the two most ferocious Viking leaders of the 9th century. Edmund mustered his army and boldly attacked Ivar the Boneless and Ubba Ragnarsson. The English were defeated and Edmund went to negotiate a peace deal with the Vikings. A contemporary chronicle records what happened next:

"King Edmund stood within the hall with Ivar, who then came, and discarded his weapons. Edmund willed to imitate Christ's example, which forbade Peter to fight against the fierce Jews with weapons. Lo! To the dishonourable man Edmund then submitted and was scoffed at and beaten by cudgels. Thus the heathens led the faithful king to a tree firmly rooted in Earth, tightened him thereto with sturdy bonds, and again scourged him for a long time with straps. He always called between the blows with belief in truth to Christ the Saviour. The heathens then became brutally angry because of his beliefs, because he called Christ to himself to help. They shot then with arrows, as if to amuse themselves, until he was all covered with their missiles as with bristles of a hedgehog, just as Sebastian was. Then Ivar, the dishonourable Viking, saw that the noble king did not desire to renounce Christ, and with resolute faith always called to him. Ivar then commanded to behead the king and the heathens thus did. While this was happening, Edmund called to Christ still. Then the heathens dragged the holy man to slaughter, and with a stroke struck the head from him. His soul set forth, blessed, to Christ."

The tale of Edmund's devotion to Christ at the moment of death was carried far and wide by his sword-bearer, who had been allowed to live by the Vikings. Edmund was at once declared a martyr and a saint. He became a sort of patron saint for those Englishmen fighting the Vikings, and in turn of all England.

St Edward the Confessor was the king of a united England who came to the throne in 1043. He ruled reasonably well, and certainly England prospered during his long and peaceful reign. He was a generous benefactor of the Church, and almost invariably took the side of the Church authorities in any disputes over land ownership or rents due. This earned him the admiration of the monks who wrote up the Chronicles and so enhanced his reputation. However, Edward failed in the primary duty of a medieval king when he failed to produce a legitimate heir. England was thus invaded first by King Harald Hardrada of Norway and then by Duke William of Normandy, both of whom had slight claims to the kingdom. The King of England who had been chosen by the English, Harold II, defeated the Norwegians but was killed by William, who then became King of England and imposed a brutal Norman rule.

Almost a century later, King Henry II was looking around for a way to unite his kingdom after the nasty civil wars of his predecessor, King Stephen. He came across writings emphasising Edward the Confessor's piety and recognised a good thing when he saw it. Edward had been English, but he was also Henry II's great great uncle. He thus represented Henry's ancestors, the old English royal family, good government and devotion to the church. Henry began agitating for Edward to be made a saint. He paid for historical research that resulted in a biography of Edward that emphasised his piety and good works, then sent it off to Rome with a request to the Pope to make Edward a saint.

The pope duly obliged. Henry was delighted and declared that the new St Edward the Confessor was the patron saint of the King of England. The anniversary of his death, 5 January, was to be a feast day throughout England. A great shrine was built inside Westminster Abbey for St Edward and visits to the shrine became obligatory for all future rulers of England — at least until it was destroyed by order of Oliver Cromwell in the 17th century.

So England had two patron saints — one for the king and one for the people — and thus things stood until the 1340s. England by then had a new king, the young Edward III. And Edward had a problem.

His father had been the weak and ineffectual Edward II who had poured wealth and political influence into the hands of his sycophantic favourites. England had been defeated in battle by the Scots (the shame of it) and torn apart by civil war. Edward had ended his life in gruesome circumstances being murdered on the orders of his wife and her lover. The royal family had fallen very low.

Now Edward inherited the discredited crown, and found himself at war with France — a conflict that would become the Hundred Years War. France was then the largest and most powerful kingdom in Europe, while England was riven by factions and almost bankrupt. Edward needed a rallying point for the war. He looked at St Edmund and saw a man who had been killed after losing a battle. St Edward was not much better, having never fought a battle in his life.

Edward needed a warrior saint. He needed St George.

When Edward had been a boy he was made a knight and was given a book in which was written advice on how a perfect knight should behave. The front of the book was adorned with a fine painting of the boy Edward being handed arms and armour by St George. On the occasion of his coronation, Edward had the chapel in Westminster Palace repainted. The wall behind the altar showed the new King Edward being led to the holy altar by St George.

Clearly St George was already a favourite with King Edward III, but the turning point seems to have come during the Siege of Calais. The English army was camped around the French town when news came that a French army was approaching determined to relieve the siege by defeating the English army. When he heard the news Edward grabbed his sword and kissed the hilt.

"Ha! By St George we will have the victory this day," he declared. The English did indeed drive off the French force and went on to capture Calais.

On his return to England for a break in the fighting, Edward founded the Order of the Garter on St George's Day, 23 April 1348. From the start the patron saint of the prestigious order was St George, and the symbol of the order is a shield bearing the cross of St George

King Edward III of England, who adopted St George to be the patron saint of England for the wars against France that began in 1337 and were to last until 1453.

surrounded by a garter bearing the words "Honi soit qui mal y pense". The motto translates as "Shame on him who thinks evil of it".

Traditionally the words come from an incident that took place at Eltham Palace in 1347. King Edward was dancing with Joan, Countess of Salisbury, who was betrothed to his valiant warrior son the Black Prince. The lady's garter suddenly slipped off and fell to the floor, causing a degree of sniggering from the watching courtiers. "Honi soit qui mal y pense", snapped the king to silence the unseemly laughter. Unusually for a medieval order of chivalry, the Order of the Garter admitted ladies as members.

King Edward rededicated the private chapel at Windsor Castle to

St George and made it the home of the new order. The Order of the Garter still exists, with the reigning monarch as its leader and members chosen by the monarch. An annual ceremony at St George's Chapel, Windsor, is held in June, followed by a meal in the castle.

It was, however, the fighting in France that really made St George into an English saint. In the days of chivalry each knight proudly displayed his coat of arms on his shield and cloak. All of his men wore clothes cut from cloth dyed the colour of the knight's coat of arms. Towns and shires that sent contingents to the royal army provided their men with outfits likewise based on their traditional colours. Cheshire traditionally sent soldiers dressed all in dark green, while London provided uniforms of red and white.

This made the English army that campaigned in France season after season, year after year a very colourful sight. Men marched in a multitude of brightly coloured clothes under a hundred or more heraldic banners. Heralds were paid to learn and know the various banners, coats of arms and outfits so that they could recognise at a glance who was who. For the ordinary soldier or knight, things were not so easy. They might know the banners or outfits of men they fought beside, but the sudden arrival of a new unit could cause consternation. More than once friends were thought to be enemies, and enemies to be friends.

To solve the problems, King Edward decided to use the badge of his new favourite saint. Every Englishman serving in France — be he nobleman, knight or archer — had to wear a small cloth cross of St George about 4 inches across sewn on to his left breast. Moreover, every English army or detachment had to carry a flag of St George in addition to whatever heraldic banners its knights and nobles might sport. Edward's favoured flag of St George for use on campaign was a square flag some five feet across. Later guidons, long narrow flags with forked tails, became more common.

Thus the English could recognise each other, and be recognised by their enemies, by the use of the cross of St George. Any Frenchmen who favoured St George as a saint rapidly lost interest as the English came to acquire a monopoly over the saint.

Edward, the Black Prince, at the Battle of Crecy in 1346. Such spectacular victories made the English the leading military men in Europe.

The stunning victories won by Edward III in France at Crecy and Poitiers enhanced the reputation of English soldiers across Europe. Many men left the royal army to earn a living as mercenaries in Spain, Italy, Germany and even further afield. Wherever they went, these men carried the cross of St George to show that they were experienced, talented English soldiers ready for hire and worth the high prices they charged.

Some of these men did very well for themselves. John Hawkwood, for instance, was born the second son of an Essex tanner in 1320. His elder brother inherited the small business, so he joined the army and went to France. He fought in the royal army until 1360 when he led a small group of soldiers to become mercenaries fighting for the Duke of Burgundy, an ally of England. In 1364 he led his men over the Alps to work for Pisa. For the next 26 years Hawkwood worked in Italy, adding Italians to his band of Englishmen to create a large and highly successful private army for hire. He was knighted, married the daughter of the Duke of Milan and in 1390 retired to Florence as one of the richest men in the city. Not bad for a tanner's boy out of Essex.

By 1400 the cross of St George was known across all of Europe as the symbol of the English at war.

In 1415 King Henry V of England took a new army to France. By this date English soldiers were wearing a sleeveless tunic of white on

The tomb of Sir John Hawkwood in Florence. The use of the cross of St George by English mercenaries such as Hawkwood made it synonymous with England across Europe.

The Battle of Agincourt in a contemporary chronicle. The English soldiers, on the right, wear white sleeveless tunics on to which has been stitched a red cross.

which was stitched a red cross. What had at first been a small badge under Edward III was now almost a national army uniform, one of the first ever used. Before he set off, Henry decreed that special prayers should be read out in every parish church to St George to ask for victory.

The prayers must have worked, for on 25 October Henry fought and won the great Battle of Agincourt. His small army of 6,000 men trounced a French force of over 30,000. The English lost about 450 killed, while the French lost over 11,000 dead or captured. Henry then married the daughter of the French king and was recognised as heir to the French throne.

On his return to England, the victorious Henry was feted as a great hero. When he reached London on 23 November, Henry led a parade through the streets. The city authorities had spared no expense, erecting triumphal arches and laying on entertainments along the way. In

Cornhill, Henry found himself facing a wooden castle "in the middle of which under a splendid canopy stood a most impressive image of St George armed, except for his head which was adorned with a laurel wreath sewn with gems sparkling like precious stones, having behind him a scarlet tapestry gleaming with his arms in a number of shields. On his right hung a triumphal helmet, and on his left a great shield of his arms. In his right hand he held the hilt of the sword with which he was girt and in his left he held a cross extended across the battlements of the castle with the words 'Honour and Glory be to God Alone'. And there was a crowd of boys representing the angelic host clad in white robes with faces gleaming with gilt paint and shining wings and the hair crowned with laurel crowns, who sang on the king's approach with sweet voices to the accompaniment of an organ."

Henry Chichele as Archbishop of Canterbury promoted St George's Day to be a national holy day within England.

Every street corner had a similar tableau to welcome the hero home. And the fountains in Cheapside ran with French wine, not with their usual water, so that everyone could drink a toast or two to the king.

The central role of St George in the victory celebrations was not restricted to London. The Archbishop of Canterbury, Henry Chichele, promoted St George's Day from being a feast day — on which monks and clergy read special prayers — to being a double feast day. This made the day as important as Christmas Day or Easter and demanded the presence in church of everyone for a specific service. Most people took the entire day off work for such holy days (thus giving us the word holiday).

The victories won by the English armies under the flag of St George made the saint popular back at home. Many organisations adopted St George as their patron saint, either relegating previous patrons to secondary place or dropping them altogether. Among the most colourful of these organisations were the various Guilds of St George that were formed in many towns and cities.

The Guilds of St George were organisations of citizens that met for religious and charitable purposes, but also included plenty of partying to ensure their popularity. Most such guilds charged annual membership fees and held fundraising events at which members paid to attend. The proceeds were spent on helping the poor, renovating churches and other good works. As a rule it was the richer citizens who were members, with the less well off attending such guild events as they were invited to. Consequently, the Guild of St George was often a prestigious organisation that allowed the more influential men and women of a town or city to meet together in informal surroundings away from the ears of the less well off.

Every Guild of St George held a special event on 23 April. Usually these took the form of the guild members marching in procession through the town to attend a church service dedicated to St George, then processing on to an inn for a feast. The processions often became great parades with the more humble folk turning out to line the route to listen to the bands, gasp at the costumes and cheer (or boo) the guild members. Free food was often handed out to the townsfolk and beer was usually on offer as well. It was all great fun, and in some places was taken much further than elsewhere.

In Norwich the guild procession involved a man dressed up as St George fighting a dragon through the streets. The dragon, nicknamed "Snap", was a wonder that impressed everyone who saw it. It was made of wickerwork covered over with cloth painted to resemble a real dragon. It had wings that could flap and a mouth that opened, then shut with a resounding snapping sound. The nostrils were equipped with brass tubes into which were placed fireworks that shot out flames, sparks and smoke in profusion. It was carried by two men, who also operated the wings, mouth and fireworks. The procession began at the cathedral, wound its way through the city streets for hours and ended up outside the city walls where the climactic battle between

St George and the Dragon ended in the inevitable death of the latter. Snap the Norwich dragon was especially famous, but similar combats between costumed actors were usual in other guild processions. Some included a damsel for St George to rescue, others did not. But they were all great fun for all involved.

During the Wars of the Roses, fought between the branch of the royal family descended from the Duke of Lancaster and that descended from the Duke of York, both sides claimed to be the legitimate user of the royal arms. To get around the confusion this would cause on the battlefield, the combatants took to using personal badges as flags and banners.

St George was pressed into dynastic politics in 1485. Henry Tudor, Earl of Richmond, claimed the crown as the head of the Lancastrian faction from the ruling king, the Yorkist Richard III. Henry was predominantly Welsh in ancestry and when he landed in south Wales he brought with him a French army loaned by King Louis XI and a band of Scottish mercenaries.

Knowing that a Welshman backed by the French and Scots was unlikely to be popular in England, Henry went out of his way to pose as an Englishman. His first action on landing from his ship was to kneel down on the dockside and pray to St George for aid in rescuing England from Richard's supposedly terrible rule. He then had his herald unfurl a flag of St George. Henry marched into England, killed Richard at the Battle of Bosworth and so became King of England.

Arriving in London, the new King Henry VII paid for a splendid new altarpiece for St Paul's Cathedral that showed himself and his royal ancestors watching St George fighting a dragon. Before long St George and the cross of St George began appearing on coins of the realm for the first time.

The high point of the late medieval English devotion to St George came in 1596 when the writer and poet Richard Johnson published a book entitled The Most Famous History of the Seven Champions of Christendom. The seven champions in question were a well known grouping of saints: St. George, St. Andrew, St. Patrick, St. Denis,

St. James Boanerges, St. Anthony the Lesser and St. David. They are the patron saints of, respectively, England, Scotland, Ireland, France, Spain, Portugal and Wales. Being an English book, Johnson's concentrates mostly on St George.

The book opens with St George being born in Coventry, son of Lord Albert of Coventry. When he grows up, George proves to be a chivalrous and brave knight. He fights a wicked sorceress and frees from her clutches the other six saints. They split up, but agree to meet again in seven years time. The book then gives an account of the lives of each of the saints.

St George is described as travelling to Egypt where he has his encounter with the dragon more or less as it was in the Golden Legend. However, Johnson makes a crucial change when he gives the rescued damsel a name for the first time. She is called Sabra and falls desperately in love with George, who is equally smitten himself. Unfortunately the Sultan Ptolemy of Egypt does not want his daughter to become a Christian and he packs her off to marry the Moslem Prince Almindor of Morocco. George sets off to rescue Sabra for a second time, arriving in time to stop Almindor consummating his marriage. George rides off with his bride back to England.

When the other champions return, they decide to raise an army to go on crusade. Each saint raises men from his own country, the English troops choosing the battle cry "To arms, to arms, with victorious George of England." The following crusade is enormously successful as the seven saints and their men either slaughter or convert to Christianity all the Moslems and pagans that they meet in the course of a lengthy journey through North Africa and Asia. George returned to England triumphant, had three sons with Sabra and enjoyed and a long and happy life before dying in a gallant battle against a second dragon.

Johnson's romance was only one instance of English writers inventing links between George and England. There were many others, some scholarly and others little more than folklore.

The villagers of Uffington in Berkshire, for instance, had a small hillock on the outskirts of their village where nothing would grow, not even weeds or grass. A local legend said that a monster had died on the hill, and its poisonous blood had saturated the ground ensuring nothing could live there. By 1600 the monster had become a dragon in local tales and it had been killed by St George.

Villagers at Brinsop in Herefordshire also claimed that the battle had taken place near their village. A 13th century carving of the saint spearing the dragon stands over the door to the church, and this may have contributed to the legend. The villagers said that the dragon lived in a small pond in Duck Meadow, just south of the church, that went by the name of Dragon Well. The fight took place in the field beside the church and the beast's body was buried underneath the church.

At Wixford an elm tree beside a crossroads was pointed out as being the tomb of St George. He was said to have been buried by the roadside and that an elm sapling miraculously sprang from his coffin.

Other tales were rather more scholarly. The fact that the Roman Emperor Constantine built a chapel over George's tomb in Lydda was taken to mean that the two men had known each other personally. As George had been a Roman officer, it was suggested that he had served on the staff of Constantine in the days when the emperor had been a general. Constantine is known to have been in Britain in 305 and 306, and possibly at other times, so it was theorised that George had also been in Britain at the same time.

Soon the citizens of various places were scrambling to suggest that George had visited their home towns during his time in England. Glastonbury Abbey was reputed to be the oldest monastery in England. Although written evidence was lacking, it was thought to have been the site of a Christian church in Roman times and to have remained a centre of Christian worship ever since. The monks of the abbey claimed that their house had been founded by Joseph of Arimathea, in whose tomb Jesus Christ was buried after the crucifixion, in about ad50. They quickly pounced on the idea that George had visited their monastery during his time in Britain as it helped to boost evidence for the ancient origins of their establishment.

He was also said to have worshipped at the Church of St Paul in the

The ruins of Glastonbury Abbey in Somerset. The monks of Glastonbury developed a spurious tale of a visit by St George to boost the fame of their house.

city of London. Like Glastonbury this is thought to have been a church in Roman times, though it did not become a cathedral until 886. The coat of arms of London had been a red shield with on it a white figure of St Paul holding the sword with which he had been martyred. Once the story of St George worshipping in London gained ground in the 14th century the city changed its arms. They now consist of a St George's cross in the upper left corner of which is a red sword to symbolise St Paul.

St George was also said to have visited York, largely because Constantine is known to have gone there. Caerleon on Usk was another large Roman army base, and George was said to have been there as well — although it is in Wales.

By the close of the 16th century, St George was riding high. His reputation had never been higher and his links to England seemed firm and secure. But St George was riding for a fall, and it was not long in coming.

Chapter 6

The Obscure Years

The Protestant Reformation was, on the whole, not good news for saints. The Protestants believed that humans should have a direct relationship with God. The idea that saints could intercede for a human was dismissed as nonsense. Some saints and martyrs were respected as having led worthy lives that served as examples of how Christians should live, but their role in theology was seriously downgraded.

Even worse, the Protestants delighted in debunking the excesses of the later medieval church. A favourite target was the Indulgence, a document issued by the Church which effectively reduced the post-death sufferings of a person by the remission of sins. In the course of the later medieval period some less scrupulous clerics took to selling indulgences for cash. The Protestants viewed this as mere corruption and castigated the Church for the abuse.

Not far behind indulgences in Protestant criticism was the trade in holy relics. A relic was an object that had been used or touched by a saint or Biblical figure and was deemed to be imbued with some of their holiness. A relic might be anything from a cup or shirt used by a saint through to the saint's skull or fingerbone. Prayers were often said to relics for the saint involved to pass on to God, and many miracles were said to have taken place in the presence of relics.

The Protestants were suspicious of anything that got between a faithful human and God. They also pointed out that many relics were of doubtful provenance. Some relics were undoubtedly what they claimed to be, but others were quite obviously modern cups being passed off as ancient ones or pig bones masquerading as those of a saint. Many relics changed hands for large sums of money, and fraud was widespread.

Unmasking false relics and debunking the more ridiculous tales about saints became something of a hobby for Protestant thinkers, and none were more assiduous than Peter Heylin. Heylin was both a cleric and a historian, teaching history at Oxford and rising to be Dean of Westminster. He wrote a steady stream of historical and religious tracts and leaflets, most of them designed to be deliberately controversial, though always based on sound research.

Peter Heylin debunked many of the stories that had grown up around St George.

In 1632 he decided to tackle St George. Heylin began with the hugely popular version by Johnson and had no difficulty in proving it to have been largely invented by the author. George's birth in Coventry, his three English sons and much else beside was discredited. However, St George fared better than some of those targetted by Heylin. The very real tomb of the saint at Lydda convinced Heylin that such a man had really existed, but he concluded that apart from the fact of his death it was impossible to know anything about him.

The debunking came at a bad time for St George. Many of the guilds of St George were being disbanded or wound up as the new Protestant thinking viewed with disfavour the religious devotions to the saint that went along with the charitable activities. In a few places the entertainment side of the guilds were taken over by the town council or by individuals, but they did not survive for long. The famous Norwich dragon, Snap, continued to prance through the streets on St George's Day until 1732, but then he too retired. His head is now on display in Norwich Castle. George was steadily slipping out of the public mind.

The Order of the Garter also went into decline. Although noblemen and soldiers continued to be appointed as Knights of the Garter, the organisation began to meet less and less. What had been regular church services and feasts became less and less frequent. After 1805 they ceased altogether.

In 1776 St George's reputation took a renewed battering from the pen of historian Edward Gibbon. In his monumental work The History of the Decline and Fall of the Roman Empire, Gibbon confused the George who was martyred at Lydda in 303 with another George. The source of the confusion was that the early sources state that St George was either born in Cappadocia or was born to parents from Cappadocia. This led Gibbon to mistake him for a figure named George of Cappadocia.

George of Cappadocia is known from a variety of sources and his life story is fairly well known, so it was perhaps tempting to conflate the two to produce a hybrid figure. Unfortunately for St George, George of Cappadocia was not an entirely savoury character.

George of Cappadocia was born in about 310 and set himself up in business as a contractor selling pork and bacon to the Roman army. His business prospered and George became a wealthy man. He was often accused of corruption in his dealings with army officers, and with supplying poor quality meat, but nothing was ever proved. He was, however, not popular with his fellow pork butchers and seems to have been notoriously mean. One colleague remarked that "George would sell himself into slavery for a cake."

By 356 George of Cappadocia was living in Alexandria, Egypt. He was not only fabulously wealthy, but was also the recognised leader of a religious faction in the Christian community. At this date there was a dispute within the Church over the true nature of Christ. One faction, known as Arians after their spokesman Arius, believed that God was the senior member of the Holy Trinity as he had created Jesus Christ the Son of God and the Holy Spirit. Another faction, the Trinitarians, believed that each member of the Holy Trinity was of equal status and were, indeed, but three aspects of a single deity. George of Cappadocia led the Arians in Alexandria.

In 356 Bishop Athanasius of Alexandria fell foul of the new Roman

Emperor Constantius and was banished to a remote monastery in the desert. The Arians in Alexandria moved fast and secured the election of George to be the new bishop. George at once began to consolidate his position by a savage purge of Trinitarians. Not only were his theological opponents removed from office, but many of them found themselves thrown into prison on fabricated charges of corruption and other crimes. George then began to appoint his friends to high office, and used his influence over the civil administration to divert lucrative contracts to his own business and those of his colleagues.

The ousted Trinitarians then joined forces with the pagans to raise an armed rebellion against George. The bishop fled, but returned at the head of an army lent to him by the Emperor Constantius and took back his position. Not long after, in 361, Constantius died and the gleeful Trinitarians rose in rebellion again. George was dragged from his cathedral and hacked to death, his body being cast into the sea.

Edward Gibbon was a highly respected historian, so his theory that George the Martyr had been one and the same as George of Cappadocia was widely accepted. A few historians tried to point out that the Alexandrian bishop had died some sixty years after the martyr and could hardly have a tomb if his body had been thrown away, but to no avail. It was to be well into the 20th century before Gibbon's theory was dismissed by historians. Even today some people will claim that St George was a pork butcher or a bacon salesman.

Although incorrect, the identification of St George with such a disreputable character as George of Cappadocia further undermined St George's popularity in England. By 1800 the patron saint of England was barely mentioned in polite society.

If St George was going out of fashion in England, the same was not true elsewhere. The country of Georgia has a special reverence for St George. Despite appearances, however, the name of the country is not derived from that of the saint. Instead it comes from the Persian "gurgian", which means "wolf-forest". For more than a thousand years from 645 onward, Georgia was on the front line between Moslem states south of the Caucasus Mountains and Orthodox Christian states to the north. Warfare was frequent and the area alternately independent or ruled by larger states from both sides of the religious divide. It seems to have been in the 12th century that Georgia adopted the warrior saint George to be its patron, with a number of its rulers having the name of George. In 1800 King George XII died while preparing to face a Persian invasion. He left his throne to Tsar Paul I of Russia, on condition that the Russians defend Georgia from Islam. Paul sent his army into Georgia and for the next 191 years Georgia was ruled from Russia.

A 15th century icon of St George from Georgia.
It has never been entirely clear if Georgia was named for St George,
or if the saint was adopted to match the name.

Before the Communists took over Georgia in 1919 there were 365 churches dedicated to St George in Georgia, one for each day of the year. Of these the finest to survive is the great fortified monastery at Alaverdi. Founded in about 645 by a monk named Joseph who came from Antioch to convert the local pagans, the monastery was converted into a cathedral dedicated to St George by King Kvirike the Great in the 1030s. It then remained the largest religious building in Georgia until 2004, when a new cathedral was built in the capital Tblisi.

Among the many folk tales about St George that have been recorded in Georgia is this one. Once the Lord Jesus Christ, the prophet Elias and Saint George were going through Georgia. When they became tired and hungry they stopped to dine. They saw a Georgian shepherd man and decided to ask him to feed them. First, Elias went up to the shepherd and asked him for a sheep. After the shepherd asked his identity Elias said that, he was the one who sent him rain to get him a good profit from farming. The shepherd became angry at him and told him that he was the one who also sent thunderstorms, which destroyed the farms of poor widows. After Elias, Jesus Christ himself went up to the shepherd and asked him for a sheep and told him that he was God, the creator of everything. The shepherd became angry at Jesus and told him that he is the one who takes the souls away of young men and grants long lives to many dishonest people. After Elias and Christ's unsuccessful attempts, St George went up to the shepherd, asked him for a sheep and told him that he is Saint George whom the shepherd calls upon every time when he has troubles to protect him from all evil. The shepherd fell down on his knees and adored him and gave him everything.

Continuing the link to shepherds is the Orthodox tradition that St George is a special protector of those who care for sheep. In Bulgaria St George's Day is traditionally a reason for a great family feast in rural areas. A sheep is roasted whole and shared between the members of the family. The day is also celebrated by the army which since 1880 had held an annual parade in the capital Sofia, followed by a meal of roasted lamb.

A Btr60 armoured personnel carrier taking part in Bulgaria's annual Army Day parade. St George is the patron saint of the Bulgarian Army.
Kiril Kapustin

The Keralese Christian Church in India claims to be descended from Christians converted in about ad50 by the apostle St Thomas. For more than a thousand years, Christianity in Kerala developed separately from elsewhere and developed some distinctive features. The veneration of St George seems to have been introduced by Portuguese settlers in the 1580s. Today the largest church of St George is at Puthupally, the centre of a huge parade and pilgrimage on St George's Day each year.

In Italy, Saint George is patron saint of Locorotondo, Genoa, Milan, Ferrara and Reggio Calabria. In Ferrara there was a legend that the dragon lived in the River Po. Saint George is the patron saint of Beirut, Lebanon, and of Malta.

In Belgium, St George is the centrepiece of a great festival held on Trinity Sunday in the city of Mons. The church just off the Grand Place claims to have a relic of St George, though it has been kept locked in a box so that nobody can be certain what part of his body it is. The city also houses the relics of St Waudru, who founded the city as an abbey in 656. When the Black Death threatened to engulf the city in 1349, the relics of the two saints were paraded through the streets and the plague receded. The event is commemorated to this day as a golden coach hauls the relics through the streets, then back to St Waudru's Church. Once the relics are safely back in place, the citizens pour into the Grand Place to watch a combat between a man dressed as St George and a 30 foot long wickerwork dragon operated by 19 men. The end of the dragon's tail is made up of long tufts of loosely attached hair. It is considered good luck to be able to grab a hair from the tail during the battle. For an hour or more, to the accompaniment of a rhythmically beating drum, the knight and dragon circle each other, lashing out at each other. Finally, St George kills the dragon and everyone goes home.

Bizarrely, given St George's role in inspiring the crusaders, the Moslems have had a place for him. The Moslems who lived near Lydda believed that the man buried in the crumbling tomb inside the collapsing Christian church had been a great healer. He was reckoned to be particularly effective at curing mental illness, so anyone deemed mad was brought to the church and made to lie with his head touching the tomb.

A version of the martyrdom of St George entered Islamic literature. In this version, George was a rich Moslem merchant living in Mosul, now in Iraq, in the days before that city converted to Islam. The ruler of the city, Dadan, decided to erect a huge statue to his pagan god and to force everyone in the city to bow down and worship the god. George, of course, refused and was executed. His brave death and clear preaching of Islam prepared the way for the conversion of the city soon after. Different versions of the tale appear in many different medieval Islamic texts, but all agree he was a martyr for the Islamic faith in Mosul.

Meanwhile, in England, things were about to get better for St George. The change, however, did not begin in England itself.

Chapter 7

St George Resurgent

-It seemed as if St George had become something of an embarrassment to England. A corrupt bacon salesman was not much of a patron saint, and he was gradually sidelined and forgotten. The process was exacerbated by the government's policy of downplaying the national identities of the British. Official references to England, Wales, Scotland or Ireland were removed or downplayed. Instead the counties and cities assumed new importance and Britain itself became the new nation. The Parliaments were amalgamated into a single Parliament sitting in London. The monarch was no longer referred to as the King of England, King of Scotland and King of Ireland, but became King of the United Kingdom.

The first official recognition of St George for a long time came in 1818. At the end of the Napoleonic Wars in 1815 Britain had annexed the Ionian Islands, which had been grabbed by France from Venice during the wars. The British valued the islands as naval bases in the eastern Mediterranean, and made Corfu the seat of the Governor. The new governor, Sir Thomas Maitland, sought to find some common link between himself and his Greek subjects, and came across St George. The saint, it turned out, was rather popular on the island. The Anglican parish church built for the British residents was swiftly dedicated to St George and the Governor's mansion was dubbed the Palace of St George.

Coincidentally, King George IV was looking for a way to reward the

The Palace of St George on the island of Corfu. The palace was named to emphasise the links between England and Corfu, where St George was a much venerated saint.

men working for him in the Eastern Mediterranean. He hit upon the idea of creating a new order of chivalry named after saints linked to both Britain and the eastern Mediterranean. He followed Maitland's lead in choosing St George, and added St Michael, the archangel. The Order of St Michael and St George proved to be a useful way of honouring those who have worked hard for Britain overseas. It is now usually awarded to diplomats or staff in the Foreign Office.

Also under King George IV, Britain reformed its coinage. Among the new coins introduced was the sovereign, a gold coin worth £1 that contained a quarter of an ounce of gold. The Royal Mint hired the talented cameo and medal engraver Benedetto Pistrucci to produce designs for the new coins. For the sovereign, Pistrucci produced an image of St George and the Dragon.

Pistrucci abandoned the medieval armour in which St George was usually portrayed and instead showed him as a Roman cavalryman.

The portrayal of St George and the Dragon by Benedetto Pistrucci that has appeared on British gold coins since 1816 and occasionally on silver coins as well.

In the Pistrucci version, St George was shown wearing Roman helmet and cloak and wielding a Roman sword, but was otherwise quite naked. The dragon was shown lying prostrate beneath the hooves of the prancing steed. The design was later used on the half sovereign coin as well as on the sovereign. Both coins continue to be minted to the present day.

The resurgence of St George under King George IV proved to be a mere flash in the pan. He remained neglected for most of the 19th century.

Towards the end of the century there was a marked upsurge in interest in old rural ways among the urban middle classes of Britain. In part this was driven by historical interest, but also by a concern for the urban poor who lived in often insanitary conditions very different from the open air and countryside of their rural ancestors. Maypole dancing, morris dancing and a host of other rural activities were revived and begun anew.

Poor old St George benefitted only mildly from this interest. In 1900 the Mayor of Tiverton organised public amusements for St George's Day, but the following year the new mayor did not repeat the event.

In 1894 the Royal Society of St George was founded to preserve and enhance English traditions. It was granted a Royal Charter stating that it was to:

- To foster the love of England and to strengthen England and the Commonwealth by spreading the knowledge of English history, traditions and ideals.

- To keep fresh the memory of those in all walks of life, who have served England or the Commonwealth in the past, to inspire leadership in the future.
- To combat all activities to undermine the strength of England or the Commonwealth.
- To further English interest everywhere to ensure that St. George's Day is properly celebrated and to provide focal points all the world over where English men and women may gather together.

This venerable and successful society is still going and has a website on www.royalsocietyofstgeorge.com.

Rather more successful in getting St George in front of a mass audience was the adoption of St George as the patron saint of boy scouts in 1908. The scouting movement was set up by retired military hero Sir Robert Baden-Powell to encourage boys (and later girls) to take up a more active lifestyle and to enjoy the sorts of outdoor pursuits that he had enjoyed as a young boy and later had found useful in his military career.

The huge success of the scouting movement brought St George out of obscurity and placed him fully in view of a whole new generation of youngsters. Much of the literature produced by the early scouting movement about St George was wildly inaccurate. It was, for instance, stated that St George had been the favourite saint of King Arthur and the Knights of the Round Table because he was the only saint who rode a horse. Despite this lack of accuracy, St George was portrayed as a brave, resourceful and courageous soldier whose example should be emulated.

St George was on his way back.

It was, however, to be a long haul. During the First World War, St George routinely featured on recruitment posters for English regiments. He was shown both on foot and on horse, but always victoriously despatching a rather Germanic looking dragon. After the war, St George featured in a number of advertisements promoting various products as being wholesome and English. He was also shown

The Memorial to the Cavalry of the British Empire in London s Hyde Park takes the form of a bronze sculpture of St George standing over a slain dragon.
Ian Bruce

in truly heroic pose on the war memorial erected to the British cavalry regiments in Hyde Park, London. Mounted on a splendid war horse and dressed in later medieval armour, he is shown flourishing his sword while the defeated dragon lies dead beneath his horse.

In 1940, the opening phases of the Second World War came to an end at Dunkirk. The British army that had been sent to the continent, along with thousands of French soldiers, were trapped in a small pocket around the French port by vastly superior numbers of German panzers and soldiers. While the German air force, the Luftwaffe, pounded the trapped men from the air, and the panzers launched assault after assault on the defensive perimeter, the Royal Navy moved in to evacuate the army. A key problem proved to be the shallow water off the coast. The destroyers and other naval ships could not get in close enough. The Navy then collected hundreds of yachts, barges, ferries and other shallow-draught boats to cross over the Channel to collect the men off the beaches and bring them out to the navy ships. Many of the "little ships" as they became known were manned by their civilian crews, and quite a few were sunk.

The successful evacuation from Dunkirk meant that Britain still had an army with which to face up to Hitler. Although it was a humiliating evacuation and defeat, Dunkirk allowed Britain to continue to defy the Germans. In recognition of the scale of the evacuation and the heroics of those involved, a special Dunkirk Jack was authorised. Any ship, boat or other craft that took part in the evacuation is allowed to fly a St George's flag from the bows. No other craft are permitted to fly the flag in this position.

Later in 1940 King George VI instituted two medals to be awarded to civilians who displayed conspicuous courage. The more prestigious of these was the George Cross, which is awarded for outstanding courage. It consists of a silver cross on which is superimposed an image of St George based on the Pistrucci design for the sovereign coin. The second award is the George Medal which is awarded for acts of great bravery. It is a round silver medal on which is embossed a spirited image of St George on horseback spearing the dragon.

In 1948 King George VI revived the Order of the Garter. Men and women had continued to be inducted into the order as an honour, but the various members had not met since 1805. King George organised a grand ceremony in Windsor which involved a procession of all members of the order in full regalia to St George's Chapel, a solemn service, and then a second procession back to the state apartments in the castle.

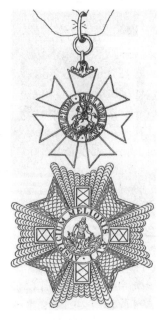

The insignia worn by a Knight Commander of the Order of St Michael and St George.

Things were not all going St George's way. In 1969 the Catholic Church announced that St George was one of several saints who was to have their feast day downgraded to being optional.

Then things began to move in a new direction. While St George was being revived as a symbol of courage and chivalry, England and the English began to feel in need of a new symbol for themselves. Since the early 19th century the official government view had been that Britain was a unified country and that the constituent nations were of less importance. In England, the largest and richest of the nations in Britain, this view had been widely accepted. Many people said England when they meant Britain and Britain when they meant England.

Then, in 1977, the Scottish national football team came to Wembley for one of the regular matches between the home teams of England, Wales, Scotland and Ireland. The Scots won 2-1 and the fans went on the rampage. Storming on to the pitch clad in tartan scarves and waving Scottish flags, the fans tore down one set of goal posts and dug up the top quality pitch to take divots home as souvenirs. The English fans and television viewers were aghast, and shocked by the anti-English attitudes of many of the Scots.

A clear difference between the English and the other nations in Britain had opened up, and was to grow increasingly wider. In Wales road signs began to be put up in Welsh rather than in English. Place names changed. Newport became Casnewydd, Cardiff became Caerdydd and Pembroke became Penfro. In 1982 a Welsh language television station began broadcasting. Plaid Cymru, a political party with Welsh independence from Britain as a key aim, began winning elections and sending MPs to Westminster. In 1979 a shadowy organisation called Meibion Glynd r, the Sons of Glydwr (a medieval Welsh prince) began a violent anti-English campaign. English-owned property in Wales was burned down and letter bombs were sent to English politicians.

In Scotland the nationalist movement was stronger and more strident. In 1974 the Scottish National Party won 11 Parliamentary seats, having taken 30% of the vote. Scots became famous for supporting "any team other than England" at international sporting events. Visitors from England found postcards showing a kilt-wearing Scot urinating on a Union Jack for sale in shops. Scottish sports teams began to ditch the British national anthem as a pre-match song. In 1990 the Scottish rugby team adopted the song Flower of Scotland, and the football team followed in 1993. The fact that the song commemorates a medieval battle in which the Scots butchered thousands of Englishmen did not go down well with the English.

By the later 1990s anti-English chants and jokes had become commonplace in Scotland, even featuring in comic strips in newspapers. Any English person who objected that the views bordered on racism was told to lighten up or that they deserved such treatment.

Unsurprisingly, the English were not impressed. They began to realise that they were not British, but English. The pace of change began to quicken.

In 1996 the European Football Championships were hosted by England. The main matches were held at Wembley, with other games played at other large stadia around the country. The opening ceremony featured a man dressed as St George in medieval armour battling a large robotic dragon. The English crowd loved it. The crowds also loved the St George's flag. Previously the only flags seen at England football games had been Union Jacks. But in 1996 enterprising flag manufacturers had flooded the shops with cheap, mass produced St George's flags. They were bought in huge numbers and waved by fans at England matches. The stands became a mass of red and white, as they have remained ever since.

The year after the Euro 96 matches, a referendum were held in Scotland to ask the people if they wanted to have a new national government and parliament based in Edinburgh exercising powers devolved from the British parliament in London. The Scots voted enthusiastically Yes. A similar vote in Wales produced a narrower Yes. In 1999 elections were held for the two bodies, and a Scottish and a Welsh government were formed.

The English did not get a national parliament nor a national government. Instead they continued to be ruled by the British government and Parliament. The fact that Scottish and Welsh MPs could vote in the British Parliament on new laws and regulations that affected only England began to cause some resentment. Another focus of disquiet in England was the Barnett Formula, a mechanism by which government spending per head is always higher in Wales or Scotland than in England. The English began to feel as if the Scots, and to a lesser extent the Welsh, were enjoying privileges and benefits paid for by English taxpayers.

In 2002 the English Democrats were founded as a political party campaigning for England to be granted the same devolved status as Scotland. The party has enjoyed mixed fortunes achieving shares of the vote varying between 1% and 12% at different elections. At the 2010 General Election the party stood 107 Parliamentary candidates, but none were elected.

Many pubs, clubs and shops began treating St George's Day as a special day worthy of commemoration in the hope of boosting sales. Greetings card companies began to produce St George's Day cards for people to send to each other. In 2006 a whisky distillery was opened in Norfolk making whisky from local, English grains. The company chose St George and the dragon for their logo. On the whole such events and initiatives proved to be successful, popular and good natured.

But there were some problems. In 2005 Tony Bennett, landlord of the Otter pub in Norfolk, applied for a late license so that his pub could stay open late on St George's Day. He had earlier opened late on Chinese New Year and other dates without any trouble, so it came as a shock when the magistrates turned the application down. "St George's Day is not a special day", he was told.

The association of England with St George, and in particular with the St George's Flag, continued to grow quickly. In 2004 the English football team qualified for the European Cup, this time held in Portugal. English fans flocked to Portugal, carrying with them thousands of red and white flags. This time the enthusiasm for the flag and for St George went further than before. Many fans began using facepaints to decorate their faces as St George flags. Fans began to be seen wearing medieval-style surcoats in white with red crosses stitched on to them. Back home in England small flags designed to be fixed to car windows appeared and for the first time sold in large numbers. At future international competitions all these features were seen more and more often. By the time of the 2010 World Cup, it was estimated that one car in four in England was flying a little flag and millions of larger flags were sold. Not a pub in England was not decorated with at least one St George's flag.

English fans at the Rugby World Cup in 2007 dress up as St George for the day. The advent of cheap fancy dress costumes has boosted such displays of patriotism.

Some churchmen have found all this secular fervour for St George rather alarming. In 2006 Philip Chester, vicar of St Matthew's, Westminster, put forward a private member's motion to the General Synod of the Church of England. It called for St George to be ousted as the patron saint of England and replaced by St Alban. Chester called the choice of George "dotty", adding "We are not at all sure George even existed, but we are sure St Alban is a real figure. What's more, he lived in this country." Rowan Williams, Archbishop of Canterbury, responded that "I think St Alban is irreplaceable in the history of English Christianity. Perhaps we ought to raise his profile because it's the beginning of the church in this country with martyrdom, wisdom and courage." The motion was defeated, but the very fact that it was debated showed how opinion in some quarters was turning against St George.

In 2008 the popular right wing politician and journalist Boris Johnson was elected to be the Mayor of London. One of his first actions was to announce that there would be official events to celebrate St George's Day, including a concert of English music in Trafalgar Square. Boris, as he is universally known, described what happened next. "The phones went wild. The emails and letters started to swamp our response teams. People started crossing the road to shake my hand, pumping it up and down and thanking me with embarrassing fervour. I felt like some Texan prospector who had idly whacked his pickaxe on some unpromising ground and then stood back in amazement before a great gusher of erupting oil."

Boris was not the only politician to notice the increasing use of St George and his flag by the English. Not all have been as positive about the change in public opinion and behaviour as the Mayor of London. One of the standard comments that politicians are prone to make is that it is time to reclaim the St George's flag from the extreme right wing of politics.

They seem to have rather missed the fact that the far right have never really used the St George Flag. The British National Party (or BNP) use the Union Jack in its logo and at meetings, as did the National Front in the 1980s. The link between English nationalism and the far right of politics is more in the mind of those on the left of the political spectrum than it is in reality.

Meanwhile, the political left have been trying to remake George according to their own agenda — effectively doing exactly what they have accused the right of doing. They have called George a Turk because he came from what is now Turkey, though in George's day the Turks had not yet arrived and he was, most likely, a Greek. They have then claimed him as an immigrant to England and proclaimed him as symbolic of a multi-ethnic society.

Most of the English who display the flag of St George see him neither as right wing, nor left wing. They see him as something much more important: the physical embodiment of England. It is the ordinary folk of England who have made St George into the football-obsessed, meat-eating, beer-drinking Englishman that he has become. And quite right too. A Roman citizen of the early 4th century would be amazed by computers, football matches, motor cars and the other paraphernalia of the modern world. And he would not recognise himself in his usual guise as medieval knight slaying a dragon.

St George has come a long way in 1700 years. We mere humans have always adapted and changed the great saint. In his day, George was a much honoured martyr who had been an important man, but who became more important by his defiance of the god Apollo and his devotion to the Christian deity. The crusaders made the soldier who defied Apollo into a knight who killed Moslems. The monk Jacobus de Voragine made the knight who fought Moslems into a celibate knight who slayed a dragon. The more worldly Richard Johnson made the celibate knight into a worldly army commander who married and produced fine English sons. Now he is being made over again. He has become a secular saint for a secular age.

And yet some features of the real St George have survived in his modern form. The values of courage, honesty, steadfastness and determination that made the original St George such a hero in his day have remained values attached to him ever since. If, as seems likely, he was a soldier then he remains a soldier in the popular imagination.

As we progress through the second decade of the 21st century it is heartening to see that St George and his symbols are as ubiquitous and popular as ever.

One other thing remains. His tomb still stands in Lydda. The church built by the Emperor Constantine has gone, so has the church built by the crusaders. The present structure dates back only to 1897, though it was built on the foundations of the medieval chancel. How much of St George's body actually remains in the grave after all these years is anybody's guess.

But the tomb is still there. So is the memory and the fame of St George.

Long may it remain so.

Index

Acre 39, 41-3
Adhemar of Le Puy 34, 36,
Agincourt, Battle of 69
Alexios I, Byzantine Emperor 34
Andromeda 57-8
Anselm of Canterbury 56
Antioch 9, 33-9, 41, 44-5, 54,
    61, 81
Apollo 9-10, 15, 17-21, 58,
    95

Basil II, Byzantine Emperor 33
Bede 47, 60
Bernard of Clairvaux 56
Bohemond of Taranto 34, 36
Byzantine Empire 32-4, 44

Canute (Cnut), King of England
    61
Cappadocia 12, 18, 20-1, 48,
    51, 78-9
Cassiopeia 57
Chichele, Henry Archbishop of
    Canterbury 70
Constantine, Roman Emperor
    11, 13-9, 33, 74-5, 95
Constantinople 28, 30, 32-4
Corfu 84-5
Crecy, Battle of 67
Crusade, First 34-9
Crusade, Third 41-3

Dadianos 20-1, 45, 56
Damerham 61
Decretum Gelasianum 25
Didyma 9-10, 15, 19
Diocletian, Roman Emperor
    8-11, 13-4, 17, 19, 24, 48,
    51
Dragon 4-6, 17, 43-54, 56-8,
    71-4, 77, 82-3, 85-9, 91-2,
    95

Edessa 33, 39
Edmund the Martyr, St 61
Edward the Confessor, St 31,
    62-3
Edward III, King of England
    63-7, 69
Egypt 8, 18, 20-1, 73, 78-9
Egyptian Life, The 18, 21

Eltham 65
England 4-6, 21, 24, 30, 41,
    45, 59-69, 72-5, 79, 83-4,
    86-7, 90-5
Ethiopia 57, 59
European Cup 92
Eusebius of Caesarea 9, 12-3,
    21

Garter, Order of 64-6, 77, 89
Gelasius, Pope 25-6, 31
George, Saint passim Genoa
    46, 59, 82
George of Cappadocia 78-9
George IV, King of England
    84-6
George VI, King of England 89
George Cross, The 89
George Medal, The 89
Georgia 59, 79-81
Gibbon, Edward 78-9
Glastonbury 74-5
Golden Legend, The 46-7,
    57-8, 73

Harham 61
Harold II Godwinsson, King of
    England 63,
Hattin, Battle of 40-2
Hawkwood, Sir John 68
Henry II, King of England 63
Henry V, King of England 68
Henry VII, King of England 72
Heylin, Peter 77
Holy Lance 36

Icons 44-5, 80
India 59, 82

Jacobus de Voragine 45, 47,
    55, 58, 95
Jerusalem 32-9, 41, 54-6

Kerbogha of Mosul 36-7

Legenda Sanctorum 46
Libya 48, 55-6
London 26, 66, 69-70, 72, 75,
    84, 88, 91, 94
Lydda 14-5, 17-9, 22, 26, 29,
    31-5, 38-9, 41-4, 58, 60-1,

64, 77-8, 83, 95

Mansur (bu Ali Mansur Al
    Hakim) 33
Manzikert, Battle of 33-4
Mary, Virgin 56
Michael, Archangel 18, 21, 85
Moscow 59

Nicaea 19, 28, 34
Nicomedia 10, 13
Norwich 71-2, 77

Oxford 26, 61, 77

Perseus 57-8
Persia 8-9, 47-8, 60, 79-80
Pistrucci, Benedetto 85-6, 89
Portugal 73, 82, 92,
Poseidon 57

Richard I the Lionheart, King of
    England 41-3
Richard III, King of England 72
Robert, Duke of Normandy
    34-6
Roman Empire 6, 9, 13, 18,
    21, 32, 78

Sabra, Princess 73
Saladin 39, 40-3
Scouts 87
Seven Champions of
    Christendom, The 72-3
Shrewsbury 61
Silene 48, 55
Syria 14, 18-20
Syrian Life, The 19, 20-1, 25,
    45

Thetford 61
Turkey 13, 94

Uffington 45-6, 73
Urban II, Pope 34

Westminster 63-4, 77, 90, 93
Windsor 26, 30, 61, 65-6, 89
World Cup 5, 93